THE RAPTURE

AND

THE SECOND COMING OF CHRIST

•

Over 7,000 Scripture References Confirming
the Truths Expounded Herein

A Book for the Classroom and the Home

•

by

FINIS JENNINGS DAKE

*Author of God's Plan for Man, Revelation Expounded,
Bible Truths Unmasked, Plan of the Ages Bible chart,
side-column notes of Dake's Annotated Reference Bible*

Dake Bible Sales, Inc., P.O. Box 625 Lawrenceville, Georgia 30246

GENERAL CONTENTS

Page

Chapter 1:

18 important terms defined and discussed   1

Chapter 2:

Daniel's 70th week and the future tribulation
for Israel and not the church—the tribulation
not to be world-wide   7

Chapter 3:

All about the future Antichrist—8 great world
empires in the times of the Gentiles—the
Common Market Nations not the 10 king-
doms of Daniel and Revelation 17

Chapter 4:

8 fallacies about the future Antichrist—no
incarnation of Satan, not Judas or some other
historic man brought back from the dead—no
world-wide peace and prosperity through
him—no computer—no personal head
wounded—the "whore" no 7-hill city—12
proofs Antichrist will not rule America or be
a world-wide dictator—12 facts about the 10
toes and 10 horns of Daniel and Revelation . . . . · 23

Chapter 5:

12 proofs Ezek 38-39 will not be fulfilled in a
war between Russia and Israel—Russia not
"the king of the north"—not a part of the 10
kingdoms of Revised Rome and Rivived
Greece—Russia not named in the entire
Bible—4 great tri-continent wars between now
and the Millennium—Russia not referred to as
"rosh" one time in the 590 times the word is
used in the Hebrew Bible—Antichrist, not
Russia, will fulfill Dan 11:44 37

Chapter 6:

Exposition of Mt 24-25—100 great events
between the rapture and the second coming
of Christ—5 proofs the rapture will take place
before all these events—28 major events of the
first day of the second advent—events of the
first 75 days after the second advent—fallacies
regarding Mt 24-25; Ezek 38-39 43

Chapter 7:

50 scriptures on the rapture—40 purposes of the rapture—10 qualifications for the rapture—the rapture not one part, one stage, or one phase of the second coming of Christ   57

Chapter 8:

Many scriptures proving a second advent before the Millennium—why the second advent is not a part, or a phase, or a stage of the rapture—the first and the second comings of God the Father to the earth—10-fold manner of the second advent—20-fold purpose of the second advent—25 incentives related to both the rapture and the second coming of Christ   65

Chapter 9:

37 fallacies about the rapture and the second advent—the rapture and the second advent proved to be "two separate and distinct comings" from heaven, the one being only a coming in the air and the other a coming to the earth—4 elects of Scripture—8 gatherings of saints, historical and prophetical, on earth and in heaven—10 historical and prophetical raptures to heaven—the times of the Gentiles   77

Chapter 10:

7 distinct scriptural proofs of the rapture of the church to heaven before the tribulation and before the coming of Antichrist—19 facts about the rapture in 1 and 2 Thessalonians— definite identification of the hinderer of lawlessness—the Holy Spirit never to be taken from the world   97

Chapter 11:

4 exclusive raptures before the second coming of Christ begins   107

Chapter 12:

The sun-clothed woman and the manchild   111

Chapter 13:

20 contrasts between the rapture of the church and O.T. saints and the second advent—all raptured saints of the first resurrection in heaven to eat a marriage supper before the second advent begins   115

MAP of the extent of Antichrist's kingdom   118

FOREWORD

Having been born in 1902 I have by now, the year 1977, had time to witness the coming and going of quite a few prophetical students who, one by one, have made boisterous claims regarding the exact TIME of the rapture, exactly WHO the Antichrist was, and exactly WHAT "the mark of the beast" would be.

Some terrified us with booklets saying "Keep this until 1927—and watch." We did and nothing happened. Others depressed us by trying to prove that going through a severe tribulation would cleanse us and purify us instead of "the blood."

One minister, for whom I conducted revival services in the 1920's listened to my sermon on "the Antichrst and the mark of the beast" one night, then left the church sick and went to bed. When I knocked at the door of the parsonage to ask about him, his wife met me with "HOW could you do that to him? Only last Sunday he told the people that 'the mark of the beast' was the fasces on the American dime and had them march up to the front to see one. Now you come along and tell them that it isn't the fasces at all!"

I have lived through strong announcements of various dictators being the Antichrist—Mussolini, Hitler, Stalin, and others. In the days of Mussolini one preacher became so convinced that he was the Antichrist that he, himself, wrote a book about it. But before the book could become a best-seller Mussolini was dead. "My God," the preacher said, "they've killed my Antichrist and I've just got 5,000 copies of my book printed!"

With all of this, and more, going on in the prophetical field during my lifetime I think that my reasons for writing this book, "The Rapture and the Second Coming of Christ" are obvious, and I trust understandable.

—Finis Jennings Dake

Chapter 1

Definition of terms used

In a study of *the rapture* and *the second coming of Christ to the earth* we must understand that there is a vast difference between the two subjects. We must also have a clear concept of the terms Millennium, the O. T. saints, the N. T. church, the future tribulation, Jews, Israel, the abomination of desolation, the judgment of the nations, the day of the Lord, the day of Christ, the end of the world, and other subjects pertaining to the latter days. The following is a brief definition of these terms as we shall use them in this book:

1. *Rapture.* The word "rapture" simply means to transport from one place to another. The Scripture terms for "rapture" are "caught up" (1 Th 4:17, 2 Cor 12:4); "receive you unto myself" (Jn 14:3); and "Come up hither" (Rev 4:1; 11:12). When we use it we mean the "catching up" of Christians to meet the Lord in the air, who then go to the planet heaven with Christ to become settled in their eternal mansions that He has gone to prepare for them who serve Him until death, or until the time of the rapture (1 Th 2:19; 3:13; 4:13-18; Phil 3:20-21; Col 3:4; Jas 5:7-8; Rev 4:1).

When we use the word "rapture" we do not mean the second coming of Christ, or any part, stage, or phase of it, for the rapture is a distinct and separate coming of the Lord with at least 7 years between the two comings out of heaven.

2. *Second Coming,* or *second advent. The first coming of Jesus* is the first time He came to earth to live here and fulfill a mission. This happened about 2,000 years ago when He died for the sins of men. *The second coming of Christ* will occur when He literally comes again to live on earth to fulfill another mission — to reign as King of the whole earth and to put down all rebellion (1 Cor 15:24-28; Mt 25:31-46; 2 Th 1:7-10; Jude 14-15; Rev 5:10; 11:15; 20:1-10; Zech 14: Ezek 38-39). The second coming is at least 7 years after the rapture, when Christ literally lands on earth to live among men as He did at His first advent (Zech 14:4-5; Dan 2:44-45; 7:9-14; 18, 22, 27; Lk 1:32-33; Mt 25:31-46; 1 Cor 15:24-28; Eph 1:10; 2:7; 3:11; Jude 14-15; Rev 5:10; 20:1-10).

Christ does not come to the earth at the rapture. He comes only as far as the clouds, and the dead and living in Christ rise to meet Him in the air to go back to heaven with Him to be with Him forever (Jn 14:1-3; Lk 21:34-36; 1 Cor 15:23, 51-56; Eph 5:27; Phil 3:21; 1 Th 4:13-18; 5:9-11; 2 Th 2:7-8; Col 3:4; Jas 5:7-8). He does come to the earth at the second advent (Zech 14:1-21; Mt 24:29-31; 25:31-46; Rev 1:7; 19:1-21).

Between the rapture and the second coming of Christ to the earth, the whole of Daniel's 70th week and the 7 years that end this age in tribulation, will be fulfilled. All of Mt 24-25; Mk 13; Lk 21:1-11, 25-36; Rev 4:1-19:21; Dan 9:27; 11:40-45; 12:1-7; Ezek 38-39; Zech 14 and many other scriptures will then be literally fulfilled. The rapture will take place *before* all these events, and the second advent will be *after* them and will end them. It will not be and cannot be until all these scriptures are fulfilled. The marriage of the Lamb in heaven will be over, as well as all the other events *before* Christ leaves heaven for the earth with His previously raptured saints and angels to fight Armageddon and begin His rule on earth eternally (Rev 11:15; 19:1-21; Zech 14:1-21; Mt 24:29-31; 25:31-46; 2 Th 1:7-10; 2:8-9; Jude 14-15; Ezek 38-39; Dan 2:44-45; 7:9-14, 18, 22, 27; Lk 1:32-33). This arrival is definitely the second advent and not the rapture. The rapture can take place *any moment* without any of the above events taking place (Phil 3:20-21; Tit 2:13; 1 Cor 1:7), but the second advent *cannot.*

3. *Millennium.* This term means 1,000 years; and it will be the first 1,000 years of innumerable thousands of years of all future eternity wherein Christ will reign on earth with God the Father, God the Holy Spirit, and all the redeemed and spirit beings who now co-operate with God to put down rebellion in earth (1 Cor 15:24-28; Mt 25:31-46; Lk 1:32-33; Rev 11:15; 20:1-10; 22:4-5; Dan 2:44-45; 7:9-14, 18, 22, 27; Zech 14; Ezek 38-39; Isa 9:6-7).

4. *Elect.* The word "elect" simply means *chosen.* Any individual or group of individuals who have been chosen of God would be the elect of God. In this sense there are may elects of God in Scripture, as we shall see in fallacy 5, Chapter 9. The word itself does not specify which elect is referred to in any particular scripture. This must be determined by each passage where the word is found and not by man's interpretation, or his own decision as to which elect is referred to.

5. *N. T. Church.* We mean by this term all the born again or saved people from the time Christ started His church (Mt 16:18; Eph 2:19-21) to the future rapture of this church from earth to heaven (Jn 14:1-3; Lk 21:34-36; 1 Cor 15:23, 35-44, 51-54; Eph 5:27; Phil 3:20-21; Col 3:4; 1 Th 2:19; 3:13; 4:13-18; 5:9; 2 Th 2:7-8; Tit 2:13; Jas 5:7-8; 1 Pet 5:4; Rev 1:19; 4:1; 5:8-10; 19:1-10).

6. *The O. T. saints.* By this term we mean the saved of all past ages from Abel to the establishment of the N. T. church at the first coming of Christ to the earth (Mt 16:16; Heb 11:1-40; Acts 7:38).

7. *The future tribulation.* This means the last 7 years of this age during which time the great whore of Rev 17 will murder saints of

Jesus (people saved after the rapture) during the first 3½ years (Rev 17:1-7, 18), and the Antichrist will murder saints of Jesus the last 3½ years of this 7-year period, known as Daniel's 70th week (Dan 9:27; Rev 12:1-18; 14:9-13; 15:1-4; 20:2-6). During the first 3½ years Antichrist will be rising to power over the 10 kingdoms inside the old Roman Empire boundary lines, and during the last 3½ years he will rule the whole 10 kingdoms. We call these last 3½ years *the great tribulation* because of being the worst time of trouble on earth that has ever been or will be (Dan 9:27; 12:1, 7; Mt 24:15-31; Jer 30; Isa 66:7-8; Rev 7:14; 12:1-19:21).

8. *The tribulation saints.* This company of saints are those who will miss the rapture and who will get saved *after* the rapture of the N. T. church and the O. T. saints, and who will die for Christ without exception in the future 7-year tribulation period between the rapture and the second advent (Rev 6:9-11; 7:9-17; 13:1-18; 14:9-11; 15:2-4; 20:4-6).

9. *The 144,000 Jews.* This special company of Jews are those in the new nation of Israel who will miss the rapture of the church but will get saved after it, in the first 3½ years of Daniel's 70th week. They will be sealed for protection from the 7 trumpet judgments (Rev 7:1-8; 9:4). They will be caught up to God and to His throne as the manchild of Rev 12:5; Isa 66:7-8; Dan 12:1. They are to be in heaven during the last 3½ years of Daniel's 70th week (Rev 14:1-5).

10. *The end of the world.* This refers to the end of this age in which we now live, which age ends at the second coming of Christ to the earth to set up His kingdom (Mt 13:39-40, 49-50; 24:3, 6, 13-14, 29-31; 28:20).

11. *The abomination of desolation.* This means the desolation of the future Jewish temple at Jerusalem accomplished by the Antichrist who will break his 7-year covenant with Israel and do away with the future Jewish sacrifices in the temple in order to establish himself as "God" in this temple (Dan 9:27; Mt 24:15-22; Rev 11:1-2; 13:1-18; 2 Th 2:1-4).

12. *Judgment of the nations.* This will be the gathering of the living nations at the second coming of Christ to determine who is worthy in each nation to go into the eternal kingdom of Christ on earth. Those who have oppressed Israel during the future tribulation will be sent to eternal hell, and those who have not will continue to live on earth as earthly natural subjects of Christ in the eternal kingdom (Mt 25:21-46; Dan 7:9-14, 18, 22, 27; Zech 14:16-21; Isa 2:1-4; 9:6-7; Rev 11:15; 20:4-6; 22:4-5).

13. *Daniel's 70th week.* This means the last 7 years of this age and is the same as the 7 years of future tribulation, during which time the

Antichrist will make a 7-year covenant with Israel. See Chapter 2.

14. *The Antichrist.* This word refers to the one man that will soon rise to power over the future 10 kingdoms inside the old Roman Empire boundary lines during the last 7 years of this age, as dealt with fully in Chapter 3. He is called the Antichrist because he will oppose Jesus Christ in most of the latter day events that will usher in the reign of God and Christ on the planet earth (Rev 11:15; 19:11-21; 20:1-10; Isa 9:6-7; Dan 2:44-45; 7:9-14, 18, 22, 27; Zech 14: Mt 24-25; 1 Cor 15:24-28; 2 Th 1:7-10; 2:1-12; Jude 14-15).

15. *The kingdom of God on earth.* By this we mean the literal earthly kingdom that God, Christ, and the Holy Spirit will establish on earth at the second advent of Christ, and which will continue on earth eternally, as stated in the scriptures of the last point above.

16. *Israel, Jews.* The terms *Israel* and *Jews* refer to the natural seed of Abraham, Isaac, and Jacob who are now the new nation of Israel in Palestine. They are being gathered there in fulfillment of prophecy, as referred to in Chapter 9, fallacy 5. For hundreds of scriptures proving that the Jews and Israelites of today are the same people, see notes in the Dake Bible called "Anglo-Saxon or British-Israel theory" beginning on page 367 of the O. T., col 1. See also page 138 of the Dake N. T., col. 4. They are not Anglo-Saxons, the British, or the American people. The terms *Jews* and *Israel* refer to the same race of people and are used interchangeably of the same people in many plain scriptures in both Testaments. All Jews are Israelites and all Israelites are Jews as proved in the notes referred to above.

17. *The wrath of God.* When we speak of this we refer to the wrath that God will pour out upon men beginning with the 6th seal of Rev 6:12-17, continuing through the 7 trumpets of the first 3½ years of Daniel's 70th week (Rev 8:1-13:18), and ending with the 7 vials of the wrath of God in the last 3½ years of that week (Rev 15:1-18:24). This wrath will be poured out upon the great whore and the 10 kingdoms of the old Roman Empire territory in the first 3½ years (Rev 17:1-18) for their murder of Jews and Christians (people saved after the rapture), and upon the Antichrist and the same 10 kingdoms who will be dominated by him during the last 3½ years (Dan 7:8, 23-24; Rev 13:5; 17:8-17). Antichrist will martyr the saints and Jews during this time. He will demand the worship of himself from all men who live in his 10-kingdom empire and will murder millions who refuse him (Rev 12:1-18; 14:9-11; 15:2-4; 20:4-6). God's wrath will be completed during the time of the 7th vial at the return of Jesus Christ from heaven with the raptured saints and angels to defeat the nations and their armies at Armageddon (Isa 63; Ezek 38-39; Zech 14; Mt 24:29-31, 38-42; 25:31-46; 2 Th

1:7-10; 2:8-12; Jude 14-15; Rev 14:12-20; 16:13-21; 18:1-24; 19:11-21).

18. *The day of the Lord.* By this term we mean the day that Christ literally comes to reign on earth with His raptured saints and angels (Zech 14:1-9). It will be His day of rule on earth, not man's day. The day of the Lord is a day of punishment for the living wicked (Isa 1:24-31; 2:1-4; 4:1-6; 9:6-7; 10:20-34; 11:3-12:6); a day of destruction from the Almighty (Isa 13:6-9; Joel 1:15); a day of God's wrath upon the enemies of Israel (Isa 13:9-13; 34:8); a day of darkness and gloominess (Joel 2:1-11, 31; 3:13-15; Amos 5:18-20; Zech 14; 1 Th 5:3; 2 Th 1:7-10; 2:7-10; Jude 14-15; Rev 19; Mt 24:29-31; 25:31-56); a day of trouble and distress (Zeph 1:7-18); a dreadful day (Joel 2:31; Mal 4:5-6; Acts 2:16-21; a day of sudden destruction of millions of wicked men on earth (1 Th 1:9; 2 Th 1:7-10; 2:7-10; Jude 14-25; Rev 19:11-21; Zech 14; Joel 3; Ezek 38-39); and a day when all the enemies of God will be put down and death destroyed (1 Cor 15:24-28).

The day of the Lord begins with the second advent of Christ (Zech 14:1) and ends 1,000 years later when the heavens and the earth will be renovated by fire (2 Pet 3:10-13; Heb 1:10-12; 12:26-28). Between these two points in time Christ will rule all nations with a rod of iron for the express purpose of ridding the earth of all rebellion (1 Cor 15:24-28). This day of the Lord is the time that Paul said would come *after* the *hinderer* of lawlessness is removed from the earth, and *after* the reign of the Antichrist. See 2 Th 2:1-12. In this scripture Paul made it clear that two things must precede the day of the Lord — a great falling away and the man of sin be revealed.

The term "the day of Christ" in 2 Th 2:2 should have been translated "the day of the Lord" as it is translated in 25 different versions. One version translates it "the day of Jehovah." This definitely associates "the day of the Lord" with the coming of the Lord to destroy Antichrist. Thus, the day of the Lord cannot take in the future tribulation and the reign of the Antichrist. It begins with the destruction of Antichrist at the second advent at least 7 years after the rapture of the church. See Zech 14:1-5.

At this point, man's rule of the earth will come to an end and the Millennium will begin. It will be the day that the Lord will begin His reign of 1,000 years to put down all rebellion and all enemies under His feet (1 Cor 15:24-28).

Paul expresses the idea of "the day of the Lord" this way: "Then cometh the end, when he shall have delivered up the kingdom to God, even the Father; when he shall have put down all rule and all authority and power. For he must reign (for the 1,000 years of Rev 20: 1-10), till he hath put all enemies under his feet. The last enemy that shall be destroyed is death. For he hath put all things under his feet. But when he saith, all things are put under him, it is manifest that he is excepted, which did put all things under him. And when all things shall be subdued unto him, then shall the Son also himself be subject unto him that put all things under him, that God may be all in all" (1 Cor 15:24-28).

At this time—when all enemies are put down and death is destroyed—the heavens and the earth will be purified by fire and the new heavens and the new earth will begin (Isa 65:17; 66:22-24; 2 Pet 3:10-13; Heb 1:10-12; 12:25-28; Rom 8:14-25; Rev 21:1-22:5). Also at this point—when He will reign, being supreme over this rebellious part of His kingdom again—"the day of God" will be ushered in (2 Pet 3:10-13). The kingdoms of this world will then truly become the kingdoms of God, Christ, the Holy Spirit, and all the faithful saints and angels (Rev 11:15).

Chapter 2

Daniel's 70th Week and the Future Tribulation

To understand the books of Daniel and Revelation and related scriptures such as Mt 24-25; Mk 13; Lk 21; 2 Th 2, and especially to understand the time of the rapture and the second advent, one must clearly understand the 70 weeks of Dan 9:24-27. Without doubt, all the above scriptures will be fulfilled during the last 7 years of this age known as "Daniel's 70th week." It must be understood, if we want clear truth, that Israel, and not the church, is the one dealt with in the 70th week, for Israel only was the one dealt with in the first 69 weeks. All the 69 weeks were literally fulfilled with Israel before the church age began. Not once was the N. T. church mentioned in their fulfillment (Dan 9:24-26), and not once is the church mentioned as being on earth during the fulfillment of the 70th week of Dan 9:27; Mt 24:15-31; Lk 21:25-36 and Rev 4:1-19:21. The New Testament was not yet made and ratified by the blood of Jesus Christ (Mt 26:28) until the end of the 69th week when the Messiah was cut off and crucified (Dan 9:26). The future 70th week will not and cannot begin until the N. T. church is raptured and God again begins to deal with "thy people (Israel), and thy holy city (Jerusalem)" to do 6 things with them as listed below.

Any involvement of Gentiles in the 70th week will be their seeking to exterminate both Israel and Jerusalem from the earth. In fact, this will be the sole purpose of the nations who will come against Israel and Jerusalem at the battle of Armageddon (Isa 63; Ezek 38-39; Joel 2-3; Zech 14; Rev 19:11-21). At the return of Christ to the earth antisemitism will be banished from men forever (Isa 2:1-4; Zech 8:23; 14:16-21). All activity of the N. T. church will end before the 70th week begins, as we shall see in Chapter 7.

Daniel's 70 Weeks (Dan 9:24-27)

The expression *seventy weeks* literally means *seventy sevens of years.* If days were meant it would be so expressed as in Dan 10:3. Daniel's prayer, to which this vision was an answer, did not concern days, but years (Dan 9:2). Then, too, we know from Scripture that the last week (Dan 9:27) is divided into two parts of 3½ years each (Dan 7:25; 12:7; Rev 11:2, 3; 12:5, 14; 13:5). The whole period of "seventy sevens" is 490 years which are determined or marked off from all other years and concern only "thy people (Israel) and thy holy city (Jerusalem)," for which Daniel was praying (Dan 6:10; 9:1-23). There are 6 prophetic events to take place during these 490 years relative to Israel and Jerusalem, for 6 purposes:

1. *To finish the transgression.* The Hebrew word for "transgression" here is "pasha." It means to revolt, rebel, or sin against lawful authority. It is often translated "transgression" (Ps 51:13; Isa 43:27, etc.). This transgression has reference to Israel in her rebellion against God. This prophecy foretells the culmination of that rebellion. The law was added because of transgression until the Seed should come, and it served as a schoolmaster to lead Israel to Christ (Gal 3:17-25). Israel failed to receive their Messiah so they were broken off in unbelief from God's favor as a nation. They will not be received again fully until the second coming of Christ, who will "turn ungodliness from Jacob" and cause a nation to be born again at once (Rom 11:25-29; Isa 66:7-10; Ezek 36:24-30; Zech 12:10-13:1).

2. *To make an end of sins.* Israel's sins, if collected in the form of concrete matter, would fill the whole earth; for she has been in rebellion against God from her beginning and she will be until the fulfillment of this prophecy at the return of Christ. This "end of sins" will not be made until after the tribulation, but from that time on Israel will obey God forever (Ezek 36:24-30; 37:24-27; 43:7; Zech 14:1-21).

3. *To make reconciliation (atonement) for iniquity.* The Hebrew word for "iniquity" is "avon" and means perverseness, to be crooked, or wrung out of course (1 Sam 20:30; 2 Sam 19:19; Job 33:37). Atonement was made on the cross for the whole world, but Israel as a nation has not yet appropriated its benefits and will not do so until the return of Christ (Zech 13:1-7; Rom 11:25-27; Isa 66:7-8).

4. *To bring in everlasting righteousness.* When the transgression has been finished, an end of sins made, and the full benefits of the atonement will have been realized by Israel, then everlasting righteousness will be ushered in (Isa 9:6, 7; 12:1-6; Dan 7:13, 14, 18, 27; Mt 25:31-46; Ezek 43:7; Rom 11:25-29).

5. *To seal up the vision and prophecy.* This means to make an end of certain prophecies concerning Israel and Jerusalem. The word "prophecy" should be translated "prophet" as elsewhere. It means that there will be no further need of inspired men to rebuke Israel in an attempt to lead them into the way of righteousness "for all shall know the Lord from the least unto the greatest" (Jer 31:31-40; Isa 11:9).

6. *To anoint the most Holy.* This refers to the cleansing of the holy of holies, the temple, and the city of Jerusalem from the abomination of desolation and the sacrilege of Gentiles, and to the establishment and anointing of the Millenial temple of Ezek 40-43,

which is yet to be built by Christ at His second advent (Zech 6:12-13).

The 490 Years are Divided into Three Periods:

1. **THE FIRST PERIOD** consisted of 7 sevens or 49 years during which time the Holy City, its street, and wall were to be built "even in troublous times" (Dan 9:25). These 490 years began with "the commandment to restore and build Jerusalem unto the Messiah." There were three decrees for the restoration of the city. The first was given during the first year of the reign of Cyrus, king of Persia (Ezra 1:1-4; 3:8; Isa 44:28; 45:1-4; 46:11). Cyrus reigned 9 years, then Cambyses, his son, reigned 7 years. In the reign of Cambyses the work on the temple and city ceased (Ezra 4:1-24). Darius I of profane history reigned 35 years. In the second year of his reign he reconfirmed the decree made by Cyrus, and the work was started again. The temple was finished in the 6th year of his reign, but the city was not then yet restored although 57 years had passed since the first decree had been made by Cyrus (Ezra 6:1-6). Xerxes reigned 21 years during which time the city was not yet completed (Dan 11:1-3). Artaxerxes reigned after Xerxes for 20 years and then gave the third decree to Nehemiah to "restore Jerusalem unto the Messiah" (Neh 2:1-6:19; Dan 9:25-26). Nehemiah restored the walls in 52 days after he reached Jerusalem, but this was by no means the full restoration of Jerusalem. This restoration took place 7 sevens or 49 years after the third decree, which was given about 452 B.C.

2. **THE SECOND PERIOD** consisted of 62 sevens or 434 years. It began immediately after the first period of 7 sevens or 49 years, and continued without a break to the time when the Messiah was "cut off" or crucified (Dan 9:26). The term "cut off" is from the Heb. *karath,* to cut off in death (Gen 9:11; Dt 20:20; Jer 11:19; Ps 37:9). These 49 and 434 years make 483 years from the third decree to the crucifixion of the Messiah, or 69 of the 70 sevens of years, leaving the last period of the 7 sevens (the 70th week) concerning Israel and Jerusalem to be fulfilled sometime after the crucifixion of Christ.

3. **THE THIRD PERIOD** will consist of one 7-year period better known as Daniel's 70th week. The crucifixion of the Messiah ended the 69th week and God then ceased dealing with Israel as a nation (Mt 23:37-39; 1 Th 2:16). They were broken off because of unbelief and their city was destroyed as predicted in Dan 9:26 and by Jesus in Mt 21:43; 23:37-39; Lk 21:20-24. See also Acts 13:45-49; Rom 11. The 70th week will be fulfilled when Israel, partially gathered, will have existed as a nation in possession of Jerusalem for the first 3½ years and Antichrist will have possessed the same city part of the last 3½ years of this Week (Dan 9:27; Mt 24:15-22; Rev 11:1-2; 2 Th

2:4).

Not one of the 6 events above has been fulfilled as yet concerning Israel and Jerusalem. They must be fulfilled in the future in the 70th week (the last 7 years of this age) between the rapture and the second advent. They will parallel the 7-year covenant made between Antichrist and Israel (Dan 9:27; Mt 24:15-22). The 7-year period will be the time when all the events of Mt 24:4-31; 25:31-46; Rev 4:1-19:21 will be fulfilled, and when the whole 7-year tribulation will run its course. What is to happen during this Week was not revealed to Daniel in detail, but it was made known to John in Rev 4:1-19:21. Other details were revealed by Jesus in Mt 24:4-31; 25:31-46; Lk 21:1-11, 25-36. This Week of years will begin after the rapture of the church and continue to the second advent. The present church age comes in between the 69th and 70th weeks, or between Israel's rejection as a nation (Mt 23:37-39; Rom 9-11) and her conversion as a nation at the second advent of Christ (Isa 66:7-8; Zech 12:10-13:1; Rom 11:25-29).

The Future Great Tribulation
(Jer 30; Dan 12:1; Mt 24:15-31; Lk 21; Rev 4:1-19:21)

When we speak of the future tribulation we refer only to Daniel's 70th week — the last 7 years of this age, ending with the second advent of Christ with the raptured saints and angels to set up an eternal kingdom over all earthly nations. We must distinguish between the future tribulation of the last 7 years of this age and the ordinary tribulation that all Christians may have to endure, more or less, in every generation.

Time and Length of the Tribulation

Tribulation will begin to affect Israel before the 70th week begins. How long before is not certain, but when Antichrist rises at the beginning of the Week, Israel will be undergoing persecution by the whore and the 10 kings of Revised Rome who are to be dominated by the whore of Rev 17 until the middle of the Week. Antichrist will come out of Syria, one of the 10 kingdoms and will make a 7-year covenant with Israel assuring them of protection in their continued establishment as a nation (Dan 9:27). The Jews will not accept the great whore dominating the nations of the old world and murdering all heretics (Rev 17:6). And, because they will not submit, there will be a widespread persecution of the Jews and "they shall be hated of all nations" during the time of "the beginning of sorrows" when Antichrist will be endeavoring to conquer all these nations (Mt 24:4-12). Antichrist will need Jewish support to help him get control over these 10 kingdoms, so he will make an alliance with them for 7 years. Therefore, the time of the tribulation is to be during the whole of Daniel's 70th week (Dan 9:27). It will end at the second advent (Mt 24:29-31).

The fact that saints of the first 3½ years of Daniel's 70th week are to be killed by both the great whore and the 10 kings, while Anticrhist is coming to power, is conclusive proof that there will be tribulation for saints then (people saved after the rapture), and Jews living outside the nation of Israel during this time. It is only in the middle of the Week that Antichrist will be given power over the whole 10 kingdoms, and then he and the 10 kings will destroy the great whore making him the object of worship the last 3½ years (Dan 7:7-8; Rev 13:1-18; 17:8-17). Thus it is not true that the whole tribulation will last for only 3½ years. Only *the great tribulation* will last this length of time, as we shall see below.

Divisions of the Tribulation

1. *THE FIRST DIVISION* takes in the first 3½ years of the 70th week of Daniel and is termed "the lesser tribulation" of this week, because it is not as great in severity as the last 3½ years. In these first 3½ years Antichrist will have a 7-year covenant with Israel. In the last 3½ years he will break that covenant and determine to exterminate them (Dan 9:27; Mt 24:15-22; Rev 12). Thus, Israel's persecution in the first 3½ years will be from a source entirely different from that caused by him (the Antichrist) in the last 3½ years. The great whore and the 10 kings of Revised Rome will cause martyrdoms of saints (saved after the rapture) and Jews the first 3½ years (Rev 17:6) whereas the Antichrist and many nations will seek to destroy Israel the last 3½ years. The judgments of God upon the Roman Empire territory during the 6th seal and the 7 trumpets of Rev 6:9-11; 7:9-17 prove that there will be widespread persecution of Christians and Jews during the first part of Daniel's 70th week.

2. *THE LAST DIVISION* takes in the last 3½ years of the Week and is termed "the great tribulation" because it is more severe in persecution upon Israel than the first 3½ years. Antichrist, who will protect Israel the first 3½ years, will break his 7-year covenant with her in the middle of the Week and will become her most bitter enemy. He will then seek to destroy Israel, which will bring from God the terrible judgments of the 7 vials of the last 3½ years. This part of the future tribulation includes the fulfillment of Rev 10:1-19:21; Mt 24:15-31; Lk 21:25-36; Dan 9:27; 11:40-45; 12:1-13; Isa 66:7-8 and Jer 30. These scriptures portray the greatest time of trouble that has ever been or ever will be again.

Purposes of the Tribulation

1. To purify Israel and bring the nation back to a place where God can fulfill the everlasting covenants made with the fathers of Israel (Isa 2:6; 3:26; 16:1-5; 24:1-25; 26:20, 21; Ezek 20:33, 34; 22:17-22; Rom 11:25-29).

2. To purify Israel of all rebels (Ezek 20:33, 34; 22:17-22; Zech 13:8, 9; Mal 3:3, 4).

3. To plead with and bring Israel into the bond of the new covenant (Ezek 20:33, 34; 36:24-28; Jer 30:3-11; Zech 12:10-13:9, Mal 4:3, 4).

4. To judge Israel for their rejection of the Messiah and make them willing to accept Him when He comes the second time to the earth (Ezek 20:22, 34; Zech 12:10-13:9; 14:1-15; Mt 24:15-31).

5. To judge the nations for their persecution of Israel (Isa 16:3-5; Joel 3; Rev 6:1-19:21).

6. To bring Israel to complete repentence (Zech 12:10-13:9; Rom 11:26-29; Mt 23:39).

7. To fulfill the prophecies of Dan 9:24-27; Rev 6:1-19:21; Mt 24:15, 29, etc.

8. To cause Israel to flee into the wilderness of Edom and Moab (modern Jordan) where they will turn to God for help (Isa 16:1-5; Ezek 20:33-35; Dan 11:40-12:7; Hos 2:14-17; Mt 24:15-31; Rev 12).

Character of the Tribulation

The character of the tribulation can easily be understood in view of God's wrath being poured out upon mankind for their wickedness and corruption which will exceed that of the days of Noah and Lot (Gen 6: Mt 24:37-39; Lk 17:22-37; 2 Tim 3:1-12). Men will reject the truth until God will turn them over to the "strong delusion" of the Antichrist who will cause them to believe a lie and be damned (2 Th 2:8-12; 2 Pet 3:1-9). Even after God pours out His judgements upon men, they will still defy Him (Rev 9:20, 21; 6:2-11; 17:1-18; 18:1-24). Words cannot describe the utter rebellion and wickedness of men during this period of final struggle between God and the devil over possession of the planet earth (Rev 9:21; 11:15; 12:7-12; 19:11-21; 20:1-3).

The Tribulation Will Not be World-Wide

The theory that the tribulation will be world-wide is not stated in Scripture. On the contrary, the Bible clearly reveals that the Antichrist will not reign over the whole world, but rather only over the 10 kingdoms that are to be formed inside the old Roman Empire boundary lines, as we shall see in Chapter 3 below. Most of the judgments of the trumpets and vials are stated as being only upon a *third* or *fourth* part of the earth (Rev 8:7-12; 9:12-21), and upon "the men which had the mark of the beast" and "upon the seat (throne) of the beast and upon his kingdom" (Rev 16:2, 10, 12). However, nothing is said as to the limitation of the extent of the demon-locusts or of the devil and his wrath when he is cast out of heaven (Rev 9:1-21; 12:7-12). These could go world-wide because they are spirit-beings and are not bound by human limitations as the Antichrist will be, who will be an ordinary human ruler over the Roman Empire territory in the last days. One   thing is certain, the Antichrist cannot possibly cause tribulation in the part of the earth that he will not rule over. Since he will rule over only the 10 future kingdoms inside the old Roman Empire territory, the 10 kingdoms will be the extent of the tribulation that he will cause for Israel and for the saved men of those days.

8 Proofs that Israel, NOT THE CHURCH, will go through the Future Tribulation and the Reign of the Antichrist

Proof 1: In no scripture of the entire Bible is there a statement of the N. T. church going through the future tribulation that Antichrist will cause inside the revised Roman Empire. Even if the church were on earth in the tribulation, only that part of the church that would be living inside that empire would be affected by the Antichrist and the tribulation he will cause for Jews and saved men in his empire.

Israel and not the church will be on earth warring with the Antichrist, and will have two great wars with him in a period of 3½ years. *The first war* will be when he will break his 7-year contract with Israel and defeat them in battle and drive them out of Judea (Dan 9:27; 11:40-43; 12:1; Mt 24:15-22; Rev 12:6, 14; Hos 2:14-18; Ezek 20:33-44; Isa 16:1-5). *The second war* will be after Antichrist will have conquered the nations of the north and east of the 10 kingdoms (Dan 11:44), and then lead his armies back down into Judea, planning to exterminate Israel, thus fulfilling Ezek 38-39; Isa 63 and 64; Joel 2 and 3; Zech 14; Rev 19:11-21. The Bible plainly says regarding this last war, Armageddon, that "Judah also shall fight at Jerusalem" against these combined armies of the Antichrist. He will take half of Jerusalem before Christ and His heavenly armies appear and defeat him (Zech 14:1-15).

Proof 2: Over 2,000 years before the coming of Christ to die for us God inspired Jacob to predict that all Jews would be gathered to make a nation in Palestine in the last days when the Messiah would come. See Gen 49. It is clear from verse 1 that the whole chapter concerns "that which shall befall you (Israel) in the last days" when God sends the Messiah, "the Shepherd, the Stone of Israel" to gather them (Gen 49:8-10).

The church was not to be involved in this gathering of Israel. This prophecy refers only to natural earthly Israel with whom God made an eternal covenant to give them the land of Palestine as an eternal home (Gen 12:7; 13:15-17; 17:6-8; 26:3; 28:4, 13; 48:4; Ex 6:4-8). See Chapter 9, fallacy 5.

Proof 3: Lev 26:39-46 predicts that Israel shall be scattered among all nations and that they shall "pine away in their iniquity in their enemies' lands." Moses further told earthly Israel, the elect people of God for all eternity, that if they would confess their iniquity and backslidings and would humble themselves and accept the punishment for their iniquity, God would restore them to their original contract in their original promised land. This was to be done in the last days when Antichrist would come, after the rapture of the church, as proved in Chapters 10-11. See also Dt 28. This tribulation is called "the time of Jacob's trouble" — not that of the church — a day so great "that none is like it" (Jer 30:7; Dan 12:1; Isa 66:7-8; Mt 24:15-22).

Proof 4: Moses again, in Dt 4:25-31, gave a great prophecy concerning Israel going into dispersion among the nations because of sin, saying they would be "in great tribulation . . . even *in the latter days.*" He told them that if they would turn to God and obey Him again they would be blessed again. Thus it is clear from many scriptures that Israel and not the church is to be involved in great tribulation in the latter days.

In proof 8 we have definite scriptures predicting that Israel would go through the great tribulation by Antichrist and Gentiles in the last days (Dt 4:30; 31:17, 21; Dan 12:1, Jer 30:7; Mt 24:15-22, 29-31; Mk 13:24). This latter day tribulation upon Israel is spoken of as "travail" which a woman endures in birth pangs and it was to be upon both *Israel* and *Judah,* but not the church (Jer 30:4-7; Isa 66:7-8; Dan 12:1; Mic 5:3; Mt 24:15-22; Rev 12:1-17). It is also called *sorrows* or birth pangs (Mt 24:8; Mk 13:8) and *pains* of death (Acts 2:24). The Gr. word "odin" is translated *travail* in 1 Th 5:3 of sinners who will not escape the sudden destruction by Christ at His second advent. But of the church in the same scripture it is stated that "God hath not appointed us to his wrath, but to obtain salvation by our Lord Jesus Christ . . . we shall live together with him" (1 Th 5:9-11). The comfort and edification of the saved in this passage (1 Th 5:13) are the same as that mentioned in connection with the rapture in 1 Th 4:18.

Proof 5: The last prophecy of Moses concerning Israel said, "For I know that after my death ye shall utterly corrupt yourselves, and turn aside from the way which I have commanded you; and evil will befall you IN THE LATTER DAYS; because you will do evil in the sight of the Lord, to provoke him to anger through the work of your hands" (Dt 31:28-30). He predicted that God would scatter them among the nations and destroy them (Dt 32:19-43). Nothing is said of the church going through great tribulation. The latter day story is that God would bring Israel back to Himself *after* the church age, and that the church would not go through these times of the travail of Israel, but would escape "all these things that shall come to pass and stand before the Son of man" (Lk 21:34-36; 1 Th 5:1-11; 2 Th 2:7-8; Mt 24-25; Rev 6:1-19:21).

Proof 6: The last vision in the book of Daniel concerns "what shall befall THY PEOPLE (Daniel's people, the Jews) in the latter days" (Dan 10:14). The last chapter of Daniel begins by stating a time element as well as a Jewish element. The time referred to begins in the middle of Daniel's 70th week and the tribulation upon Israel (Dan 12:1, 7-13; Isa 66:7-8; Jer 30:7; Mt 24:15-22; Rev 11:2-12; 12:6, 14).

Proof 7: In the minor prophets we have many references to God's dealings with Israel "in the latter days" in the future tribulation and the reign of Antichrist over the 10 kingdoms of the old Roman Empire territory. *Some of the main predictions are:*
1. The coming Antichrist and his wars on Israel (Dan 11:40-43; Hos 2:14-23; Mic 5:3-15 with Rev 12:6-17).
2. The regathering of Israel, not the church (Ezek 37; Hos 3:5; Zech 10:10; Isa 11:11-12; Mt 24:31).
3. The second advent of Christ and the battle of Armageddon (Joel 1:15-3:21; Amos 1:2; 5:16-20; Obad 15-21; Mic 1:2-4; 2:12-13; 4:11-13; Zeph 1:7-3:20; Hag 1:6-9; 2:21-23; Zech 2:11-13; 3:8-10; 8:1-8, 20-23; 9:1-8, 10-12; 12:1-14:21; Mal 3:2-25, 17-18; 4:1-6).
4. The coming of the two witnesses of Rev 11 (Zech 4:14; Mal 4:5-6; Ezek 20:33-44).
5. Repentance and salvation of Israel the day Christ lands on the mount of Olives (Zech 12:10-13:1; Isa 66:7-8; Mt 23:37; Rom 11:25-29).
6. Mobilization of nations against Israel and Jerusalem, not against the church (Zech 12:1-9; 14:1-9 with Ezek 38-39; 2 Th 1:7-10; Jude 14-15; Rev 19:11-12).
7. Two-thirds of the new nation of Israel destroyed (Zech 13:9).

Proof 8: James, in Acts 15:13-18 of the N. T. quotes both Peter and Amos and proves that the church is gone from the earth during the tribulation and that God is then dealing with Israel in particular. He says, "Simeon hath declared how God at the first did visit the Gentiles, to take out of them a people (the Gentile part of the church) for his name. And to this agree the words of the prophets: as it is written, After this (after completing the N. T. church) I (the Lord) will return (to the earth), and will build again the tabernacle of David, which is fallen down; and I will build again the ruins thereof, and I will set it up; that the residue of men (the Jews) might seek after the Lord, and all the Gentiles, upon whom my name is called" (Acts 15:13-18; Amos 9:11-12).

As we have seen from proofs above God did deal mainly with Israel from Abraham to Christ, but when Christ came He officially cut off Israel and turned to the Gentiles. This was after Christ had dealt with them first and they had rejected Him completely, as their Messiah (Mt 10:5-6; 15:24; 21:33-46; 23:1-39). This is why Paul could speak of the cutting off of Israel as he did (Rom 9:25-33; 10:3, 18-21; 11:1-32). This is why Paul and others in the early church turned to the Gentiles (Acts 11:18; 13:46; 14:27; 15:13-18; 18:6). This is why God plans to deal with the Gentiles in particular until the rapture, and until Israel turns to Him again.

After the church is raptured God will continue to save both Jews and Gentiles who will turn to Him (Acts 2:16-21). When the rapture takes place though there will not be one saved Jew or Gentile left on the earth. The 144,000 Jews will get saved after the rapture and will be translated as the manchild of Rev 12:5 and be in heaven from then on (Rev 14:1-5). Multitudes of Gentiles will become saved immediately after the rapture of the church and O. T. saints, but they will not be a part of the church (Acts 2:16-21; Rev 6:9-11; 7:9-17; 14:9-13; 15:1-4; 20:4-6). They will be separate from the O. T. saints, the church saints, and the 144,000 Jewish saints, as seen in fallacy 9, Chapter 9. The primary purpose of the tribulation is to bring Israel to God at the second coming of Christ (Zech 12:10-13:9); Isa 66:7-8; Dan 12:1; Mt 24:15-22; Rom 11:25-29; Rev 12:17). Many scriptures refer to Israel in the future tribulation, but not one mentions the church as being on earth during the tribulation.

Besides the above, the fact that the 70th week of Daniel (Chapter 2) concerns Israel and not the church is additional proof.

Chapter 3

The Future Antichrist

By this term "Antichrist" we mean the one man of the future who will be the leader in opposing Jesus Christ in the last generation of this age — during the great tribulation in particular. He is the one man to whom the following points apply and who will be personally destroyed by Jesus Christ as they face each other in the battle of Armageddon (2 Th 2:7-8; Rev 19:11-21; Dan 7:11; Zech 14:1-9; Jude 14-15).

It is necessary for us to understand the scriptural facts about the Antichrist regarding the time, length, and extent of his reign in order to know the time period of the rapture and the second advent and why the church will not have to face him. We should also know where the tribulation will be on earth. We must realize that the reign of the Antichrist and the future tribulation will not be world-wide, and that men outside the kingdom of the Antichrist will not have to go through what men in his kingdom will have to endure by him.

6 Truths about the Antichrist:

1. *Who is he?* At the present time this question cannot be answered. It will remain unsolved until he, the Antichrist, personally makes the 7-year covenant with Israel (Dan 9:27). Many today, as ever, are speculating on who he will be. Much harm has been done to the subject of prophecy by this, and many thinking people have turned against the inspiration of prophecy by just such unfounded speculation.

One thing we do know for sure and that is he will not be any man of the past who has died, for he is yet to be "slain" at the second advent of Christ (Dan 7:11; 2 Th 2:7-8; Rev 19:20) — and no man will die more than once (Heb 9:27). He, therefore, could not be Nimrod, Nero, Judas, or any of at least 35 men of the past whom various Bible scholars have already chosen for us as the Antichrist, many of whom have ruled the Egyptian, Assyrian, Babylonian, Medo-Persian, Grecian, and Roman empires in the past. Nor could he be any man of recent history — Mussolini, Hitler, Stalin, Roosevelt, or any other who has died. And, he cannot be Kissinger or any one of a "new crop of Antichrists" being named by some of today's so-called prophetical scholars who are making the same mistake many others have made in the past. Another thing we know for sure is that the future Antichrist will not come or be revealed until AFTER the 10 kingdoms are formed inside the Roman Empire territory (Dan 7:7-8, 23-24), and AFTER the rapture of the church, as proved by many scriptures in Chapters 10-11 below.

2. *From where does he come?* This question is fully and clearly answered in the book of Daniel, as we can see from a brief summary of the prophecies of Dan 2, 7, 8, 9, and 11 as follows:

The Babylonian Empire

In Dan 2 and 7 we have two visions that cover the Gentile world powers from Daniel's day to the second coming of Christ. The "head of gold" on the image (Dan 2:32, 35, 38) and the "lion" (Dan 7:4, 12, 17) symbolize Babylon, Nebuchadnezzar's kingdom (Dan 2:37-38; Jer 15:4; 24:9; 25:11-12; 29:18).

The Medo-Persian Empire

The "breast and arms of silver" on the image (Dan 2:32-39), and the "bear" (Dan 7:5, 12,17) and the "ram" (Dan 8:5-25) symbolize Medo-Persia, which followed Babylon in the punishment of Israel (Dan 2:39; 5:24-31; 6:1-26; 8:1-2, 20; 10:1-20; 11:1-3; 2 Chr 36:22; Ezra 1:1-3).

The Grecian Empire

The "belly and thighs of brass" on the image (Dan 2:39), and the "leopard" (Dan 7:6, 12, 17), and the "he goat" (Dan 8:5-25) symbolize the old Grecian Empire of Alexander the Great that followed Medo-Persia in "the times of the Gentiles" (Dan 2:39; 8:20-21; 11:1-4).

The Roman Empire

The "legs of iron" on the image (Dan 2:33-35, 40) and the non-descript "beast" (Dan 7:7-8, 17-27) symbolize the old Roman Empire that followed the Grecian Empire and its four divisions in the persecution of Israel (Dan 2:40; 7:23-25; 9:26; Lk 2:1; Jn 11:48; Mt 24:1-2; Acts 16:21; 22:25-29).

The Revised Roman Empire

The "feet and toes" of iron and clay on the image (Dan 2:33-35, 41-44) and "the ten horns" on the non-descript beast (Dan 7:8-24) symbolize 10 kings who will head 10 separate governments from 10 separate capitals inside the old Roman Empire territory in the days of the coming of Christ to the earth (Dan 2:31-44; 7:23-25; Rev 12:3; 13:1-18; 17:8-17). Men call these 10 kingdoms the Revived Roman Empire, but actually there will be no such thing as a "revived" Roman Empire. This would require the Roman territory to be formed into only one empire again and be ruled by one man from

Rome instead of 10 kingdoms being formed. But this the Bible does not teach. It shows that, as stated above, there will be 10 kingdoms formed inside the old Roman territory ruled by 10 kings (Dan 2:44; 7:7-8, 23-24; Rev 17:8-17). This is the next phase of the fulfillment of prophecy concerning the world empires between Daniel's day and the Millennium. It is better to call these 10 kingdoms the "Revised Roman Empire," for the old Roman Empire will be definitely revised from one vast empire into 10 kingdoms.

The Common Market Nations not the 10 Kingdoms

The popular theory of today that the Common Market Nations are the fulfillment of Dan 7:7-8, 23-24; Rev 13:1-5; 17:8-17, is false. There is not to be a United States of Europe but rather 10 united kingdoms of Europe, Asia, and Africa from the whole of the Roman Empire territory. *Note the following:*

1. The 10 future kingdoms of revised Rome are to be a political union, not a commercial union (Dan 7:7-8, 23-24; Rev 13:1-5; 17:8-17).

2. There are presently about 25 governments inside the Roman Empire territory that must be brought down to 10 kingdoms and these will take in all of that territory, not just a part of it (Dan 7:23-24).

3. The 10 kingdoms, when they are formed, will take in parts of three continents – Europe, Asia, and Africa – and not be 10 nations of Europe only.

4. It is predicted in Dan 8 that 4 of the 10 kingdoms inside the Roman Empire would be located inside the old Grecian Empire territory. Not one of the Common Market nations is from the old Grecian Empire of Alexander the Great.

The Revived Grecian Empire

Daniel did not see a "little toe" growing out of the 10 toes of the feet in Dan 2, or one from their midst plucking out three of the 10 toes. But in Dan 7 he did see a "little horn" growing out of the 10 horns, which plucked up three of the horns by the roots (Dan 7:7-8, 20-25). It is explained in these verses that one horn from among the 10 will rise to power over three of the 10. The "four wings" and the "four heads" on the leopard symbolize the four divisions of the old Grecian Empire of Dan 7. The "four horns" and the "four winds" of Dan 8:8 also symbolize these four divisions which today would be called Greece, Turkey, Egypt, and Syria. It is plainly stated in Dan 8:9 that "out of one of them came forth the little horn" or the Antichrist of the last days. The Grecian Empire will be *revived* whereas the Roman Empire will be *revised* into 10 kingdoms.

After the 10 kingdoms are formed inside the Roman Empire territory and have existed a "short space" independent of the Antichrist (Dan 7:7-8, 23-24; Rev 12:12; 17:10), he will then come out of Syria and in the first 3½ years of Daniel's 70th week will conquer Greece, Turkey, and Egypt thus reviving the old Grecian Empire territory into one empire. By this time the other six kingdoms of the 10 will submit to him without any further war (Rev 17:8-17). This will give him all the 10 kingdoms of the old Roman Empire area and they will become the 8th kingdom of Rev 17:8-11.

This kingdom is the one head of the 7 on the beast that was wounded to death, and its deadly wound was healed — of Rev 13:3, 12, 14. It must be remembered that it was one of the 7 heads on the beast that was wounded or destroyed and that came back to life again, and not the personal Antichrist or the beast itself. The heads symbolize kingdoms, not personal kings. It was one of the 7 heads symbolizing the 7 world empires which would precede the 8th kingdom or the kingdom of the Antichrist. The head that was wounded was one of the first five empires that had fallen before John wrote the Revelation. When it is revived it will be the 8th kingdom or the Grecian Empire revived (Rev 17:8-17).

In Dan 8:7-9, 23-24 it is revealed that Antichrist will come from one of the four divisions of the old Grecian Empire, these being four of the 10 kingdoms of Dan 7. In Dan 11 it is revealed that he is coming from the Syrian division of the old Grecian Empire. The purpose of Dan 7 over Dan 2 is to show additional events in the 10 kingdoms of the 10 toes and 10 horns in the latter days, and to make it clear that Antichrist will definitely come from one of the 10 kingdoms. The purpose of Dan 8 over Dan 7 is to narrow down the coming of the Antichrist geographically from 10 kingdoms to 4 kingdoms so that we can better identify the exact country that he will come from. If we did not have Dan 8 we could teach that he will come from any one of the 10 kingdoms of the Revised Roman Empire, but we would not know which one. Now with Dan 8 we can be assured that he will come from one of the four divisions of the old Grecian Empire — Greece, Turkey, Egypt, or Syria. If we did not have Dan 11 to narrow down the coming of Antichrist geographically from 4 kingdoms to only one of the four, we would be uncertain about which one of the four he will come from. As it is now, we have no grounds for uncertainty.

Dan 11 reveals war between Medo-Persia and Greece, and then the division of Greece into 4 kingdoms (Dan 11:1-4). Dan 11 also reveals that the only two of these 4 kingdoms, the king of the south (Egypt), and the king of the north (Syria) were to war with each other, off and on, over a period of years. They did war with each other for about 150 years, ending with Antiochus Epiphanes who reigned about 165 B.C. After these predictions of Dan 11:5-34 the prophet skips over to "the time of the end," showing the last day war between the king of the south (Egypt), and the king of the north (Syria), with the result that the king of the north will be the final victor over the king of the south (Dan 11:35-45).

This definitely identifies *the king of the north* to be the future Antichrist. He is the same man as the "little horn" of Dan 7 and 8; the "prince that shall come" of Dan 9:26-27; the "son of perdition" and the "man of sin" of 2 Th 1:1-12; and "the beast" of Rev 13:1-17:17; 19:11-21.

We can definitely and scripturally declare with the full authority of God's Word that the Antichrist will come from Syria, not Greece, Turkey, Egypt, the Vatican, Italy, France, Spain, Germany, Russia, Poland, England, Scandinavia, China, Japan, India, the United States, or any other part of the world outside of Syria.

3. *When is he to be revealed and come into prominence in world affairs?* This question is also clearly answered in Scripture:

(1) In Dan (7:7-8, 24 it is written that he will come "after" the 10 kingdoms are formed and after they exist a "short space" or "short time" (Rev 12:12; 17:10).

(2) Antichrist cannot be revealed until "after" the rapture, as proved in 2 Th 2:7-8, and Chapter 10, proof 1.

(3) Antichrist cannot be known in the world as such until he comes after the rapture and makes a 7-year covenant with Israel (Dan 9:27). Then, and then only, can anyone be definitely sure that this is the man.

4. *How long is he to reign?* He will rise from Syria at the beginning of Daniel's 70th week, and in 3½ years will conquer Greece, Turkey, and Egypt (Dan 7:7-8, 23-24; 12:7). At this point he will be given power over the whole 10 kingdoms and will reign over them the last 3½ years of the Week (Dan 7:25; 9:27; 12:7; Mt 24:15-22; Rev 13:5).

5. *Where is he to reign?* He is called "king of Babylon" in Isa 14:1-7 and no doubt will reign from there during the first 3½ years of his rise to power over the 10 kingdoms. He will then conquer Israel and reign from Jerusalem during part of the last 3½ years of this Week (Dan 9:27; 11:45; 12:1-7; Mt 24:15-22; Rev 11:1-2; 13:12-18). During most of this last 3½ years he will be away from Jerusalem leading his armies personally against the vast armies in the north and east of the 10 kingdoms (Dan 11:44). THIS IS THE TIME – AND NOT BEFORE – THAT RUSSIA, being one of the nations north of the 10 kingdoms, WILL COME INTO THE PICTURE and, at that time, be at war with the Antichrist. After conquering these other nations north and east, and toward the end of this Week, Antichrist will find Jerusalem in control of the Jews again. He will

then invade Israel another time hoping to exterminate the Jews but will be defeated by Christ and Israel at Armageddon (Ezek 38-39; Zech 14:1-15; Dan 11:45; 2 Th 1:7-10; Jude 14-15; Rev 19:11-121).

6. *Will he be a real person?* The Antichrist is to be a real human being and not a system or the successive head of some system. He will be a man (Rev 13:18). He will possess the talent and leadership of many previously gifted conquerors and leaders. In addition to these natural gifts, he will be endued with the power of Satan in the exercise of these gifts until the world will wonder after him and even many will worship him as God (Dan 8:22; 11:38; 2 Th 2:4, 8-12; Rev 13:1-18; 14:9-11; 15:1-4; 20:4-6). He will die a physical death as other men do (Dan 7:11; 2 Th 2:7-8; Rev 19:19-21; 20:10).

Chapter 4

8 Fallacies about the Future Antichrist

FALLACY 1: The Antichrist will be an incarnation of Satan.

TRUTH: The above cannot possibly be true because the Devil is always a separate person, a third person, working with the personal human Antichrist, and the personal human false prophet. These will never be incarnated one in another, but will act as three separate individuals co-operating together in all of their activities as seen in both Daniel and Revelation. It says in the Bible: "I saw THREE (not two) unclean spirits like frogs come out of the mouth of the dragon (Satan, Rev 12:9); and out of the mouth of the beast (a man, Rev 13:18); and out of the mouth of the false prophet (another man, Rev 13:11; 19:20; 20:10)." They will go forth to gather the nations to the battle of Armageddon (Rev 16:13-16). In Rev 13:2 the dragon gives to the beast — a separate person from himself — his power, throne, and great authority. In Rev 19:20 and 20:10 the Devil, the Antichrist, and the false prophet are seen as three separate and distinct persons who will be in two different places for 1,000 years. Thus, fallacy number 1 is to be rejected.

FALLACY 2: Antichrist will be Judas resurrected from the dead. He will be the mystery of iniquity — a supernatural man, a superman, the personal son of Satan, and a man absolutely different from all others that ever lived or ever will live on earth.

TRUTH: The theory that Antichrist will be "the mystery of iniquity" or Satan manifest in the flesh as Jesus was "the mystery of godliness," or God manifest in the flesh; that the Antichrist will be "the son of perdition" or "the son of Satan" by a woman as Jesus was "the Son of God" by a woman; and that Antichirst will be the opposite of Christ in every detail is not taught in Scripture. Not one statement about him indicates mystery or teaches that he will be a supernatural, or an immortal man from the abyss, an incarnation of the Devil, or a natural son of the Devil, as we shall see below.

The phrase "mystery of iniquity" literally means the invisible spirit of lawlessness, or the evil spirit forces that cause men to sin (Jn 8:44; 14:30; Eph 2:1-3; 6:10-18; 1 Jn 3:8; 2 Cor 4:3-4). Those who say that Antichrist is the mystery of iniquity teach that he is the beast in the abyss and will come out again as the Antichrist, this spirit being Judas who will be reincarnated. Their main claim is that Judas and Antichrist are both called "the son of perdition" (Jn 17:12; 2 Th 2:1-4). But no human being ever goes into the bottomless pit, and therefore, Judas could not be in the pit to come out later. The abyss is a special prison under the earth for demons and certain fallen angels (Lk 8:31; Rev 9:1-21; 11:7; 17:8; 20:1-3). The expression "the son of perdition" literally means "the son of destruction," and refers to both Judas and Antichrist because both are destined to destruction, not because they are natural sons of Satan by women.

In the Greek it reads "the son of the destruction" just as it reads "the man of the sin." This last phrase does not limit the Antichrist to being the only man of sin and the former phrase does not limit him to being the only son of destruction. The Hebrews and Greeks called a man who was subject to a particular evil or thing, the son of that evil or thing, as "sons of Belial" (1 Sam 1:16; 2:12; 25:17; 25; 1 Ki 21:10); "child of the devil" (Acts 13:10); "children of the wicked one" (Mt 13:33); "children of the devil" (1 Jn 3:10); "children of wisdom" (Lk 7:35); "children of the world" (Lk 16:8); "children of light" (Lk 16:8; Jn 12:36); and "children of disobedience" (Eph 2:1-3; 5:6-8; Col 3:6). Also, anyone who was destined to some particular end was called the child of that destiny, as "children of the kingdom" (Mt 8:12); "children of wrath" (Eph 2:1-3); and "children of the resurrection" (Lk 20:36). And so, it would be only logical to call both Judas and Antichrist "the son of perdition" or destruction, for both are destined to destruction in hell because of their sins. To call them natural sons of the Devil is not biblical. The Gr. *apoleia* (destruction) is never translated "Satan" and it is not reasonable to intrepret the word *perdition* as "Satan" (Phil 1:28; 1 Tim 6:9; Heb 10:39; 2 Pet 3:7; Rev 17:8, 11).

The Devil was not to have a natural son such as Judas or otherwise by a woman, as some interpret Gen 3:15 to mean. The seed of the serpent here does not refer to natural birth but to men following Satan (Mt 13:38; 1 Jn 3:8-10; Jn 8:44).

This last passage (Jn 8:44) taken by some to mean Antichrist will be a natural seed of the Devil says, "Ye are of your father the devil . . . when he speaketh a LIE, he speaketh of his own; for he is a LIAR, and the father of IT." It is claimed the word "IT" refers to one particular son of the Devil, the Antichrist, but this is erroneous. The "LIE" or "IT" here refers to a literal lie, and not to a natural son by a woman. If telling a lie can be interpreted as a natural son in this passage then it could also be so interpreted in Acts 5:3; Rom 1:25; Ps 78:36, and all other places in Scripture where lies are spoken of. No person can speak a natural son into existence.

It is also argued that Judas was the only one ever called a "devil," thus proving further that he was the Devil incarnate (Jn 6:70-71; 17:12). It is claimed the definite article is used here in the Greek thus making Judas "the devil," but actually the definite article is not in the Greek here and the literal meaning is "a devil." The Greek for "devil" is *diabolos* and means "adversary" or "slanderer" and is used of other men besides Judas who are "false accusers" and "slanderers" (2 Tim 3:3; Tit 2:3; 1 Tim 3:11).

FALLACY 3: The Antichrist will bring world peace, world prosperity, a world labor union, world commerce, one world monetary system, united world laws, world religion, and world government.

TRUTH: Not one of these things will be brought about by Antichrist. As to *universal peace,* just the opposite is true according to the Bible. He will come in war to overthrow three of the 10 kingdoms (Dan 7:7-8, 23-24; Rev 6:1-2). He will continue in war for 3½ years until he conquers these three and forces the others of the 10 kings to submit to him without further war (Rev 17:8-17). He will then continue in war until he has conquered all the countries of the north and east of Revised Rome (Dan 11:44). He will then lead the nations under him hoping to destroy Israel and stop Christ from setting up His kingdom. He is to be finally destroyed before he takes all of Jerusalem (Zech 14:1-5; Ezek 38-39; Mt 24:29-31; 2 Th 1:7-10; 2:7-8; Jude 14-15; Rev 19:11-21). When the world thinks that it is going to have universal peace and they begin to say, "peace and safety" then sudden destruction will come (1 Th 5:1-11).

As to *universal prosperity,* not one thing is said in the Bible about it. Antichrist will control the riches of his own 10-kingdom empire and that is all (Dan 7:23-25; 11:36-39). Nothing is said of his control of all the money and commerce of the entire world. As to the control of world labor nothing is said about this, either. The Heb. *mirmah* translated *craft* in Dan 8:25 means to deceive, to be subtle, and treacherous. It refers to the deceptions that Antichrist will bring, his craftiness instead of improved labor conditions and prosperity in that field (2 Th 2:7-12). Satan will help him deceive much of the world (Rev 12:9).

There will be no such thing as having *control of all law making* in the world. All that Scripture reveals is that laws will be made by Antichrist in his own empire requiring all his subjects to worship him and take his brands or be killed (Rev 13:16-18). He will not and cannot make laws that will affect the whole world, for he will not be a world-wide dictator. Neither will he be worshipped world wide, or have one religion throughout the world, as we shall see in fallacy 8 below.

FALLACY 4: Antichrist will have a computer called "the beast" in which every name of every person in the world can be listed, and he will kill every person on earth who will not list his name in the computer. This "beast" will cause the whole world to worship Antichrist or be killed.

TRUTH: Even if such a computer became part of the Antichrist's program it would be impossible for him to obtain and process all the names of all the human beings upon the face of the earth in the short time the Bible allows for his complete rulership over the 10 kingdoms — 1,260 days or 42 months (Rev 13:5; Dan 7:25). And, even if he confined himself to the names of everybody in his own 10 kingdoms, he would still have big problems — getting his laws enforced and actually applying his brands to the forehead or right hand of all the persons named by his computer, in the 1,260 days or 42 months.

FALLACY 5: The Antichrist will cause world-wide tribulation.

TRUTH: Since, as proved in fallacy 8 below, Antichrist will not rule the entire world, then he cannot cause world-wide tribulation and martyrdom of people in all lands. It being that the Roman Empire boundary line takes in only England, Holland, Belgium, Switzerland, France, Spain, Portugal, Italy, Albania, Yugo-slavia, Hungary, Austria, Bulgaria, Rumania, Greece, Turkey, Syria, Lebanon, Irak, Iran, Egypt, Morocco, Algeria, Libya, and a few other small countries, then the extent of the Antichrist's kingdom and the tribulation is clear. It does not take in the rest of Europe, Asia, Australia, Japan, Indonesia, the Philippines, New Zealand, Canada, the United States, Central America, South America, and other parts of the world outside the old Roman Empire area wherein the great tribulation is centered. Martyrdom of Jews and Christians will not be world-wide, but rather confined to the Antichrist's 10 kingdoms. Neither will the plagues of the seals, the trumpets, or the vial judgments be world-wide as we have seen above in Chapter 2. The great whore of Babylon will murder the saints of Jesus (those saved after the rapture) the first 3½ years of the Week (Rev 17:1-18), and the Antichrist of the old Roman Empire territory will murder the Jews and saints of Jesus in his kingdom during the last 3½ years of this Week (Rev 13:1-18; 14:9-20; 15:1-5; 16:1-17; 20:4-6).

What will Happen to America?

Actually, nothing is said of America in the entire Bible. We know that the U.S.A. is NOT "beyond the rivers of Ethiopia" referred to in Isa 18; that she is NOT the white horse rider of Rev 6:1-2; that she is NOT the false prophet of Rev 13:11-18; 19:20; 20:10; that she is NOT identified by the letters in the middle of the word "Jer-USA-lem"; and that she is not once identified otherwise in the entire Bible. The main concern of God regarding nations, throughout Scripture, is the final rescue of Israel from being totally destroyed and the accomplishment of her final and eternal restoration to her own land under the Messiah. One thing is certain about the U.S.A. —

it will work out its own salvation as will other countries, and they all will exist together in the eternal kingdom of God and Christ (Rev 11:15; 20:4-6; 22:4-5; Lk 1:32-33).

FALLACY 6: The personal Antichrist will be wounded to death by a sword wound in the head. He will be miraculously healed and will become an immortal man. This will make the world to wonder after him and even worship him.

TRUTH: This is completely groundless. It was not the human Antichrist that would receive the wound by the sword and live again. It was one of the heads on the beast that was wounded to death and was to be revived again as the 8th kingdom. The 7 heads on the beast are 7 kingdoms (Rev 17:9-10). The beast, itself, is the 8th kingdom (Rev 17:11). Five of these 7 kingdoms had already fallen before John's day; only one was in existence in John's day; and the 7th was yet to come. The beast had been on earth before John and would become the 8th kingdom after him (Rev 17:11). This refers to the overthrow of the old Grecian Empire, the 5th kingdom that had fallen before John, and to its revival again as the 8th kingdom by the future Antichrist (Dan 8:8-25; Rev 13:1-2; 17:11). The human Antichrist, the head of the 8th empire, will never be killed and resurrected from the dead to become a supernatural or resurrected person. It is plainly stated in Dan 7:11; 2 Th 2:7-8; Rev 19:20 that the personal human Antichrist will be killed at the second advent of Christ, and so he will be an ordinary mortal man all the days of his reign on earth. The 8 kingdoms are: Egypt, Assyria, Babylon, Medo-Persia, Greece (the 5th that had fallen before John), Rome (the 6th that was in existence in John's day), Revised Rome (the 7th made up of the 10 kingdoms yet to come inside the old Roman Empire territory), and Revived Grecia (the 8th kingdom yet to come). The 5th was the old Grecian Empire which was wounded to death. In its revival again as an empire by the Antichrist (Revived Grecia) it will be the head wounded to death that will be healed and not the human Antichrist (Dan 7:6; 8:8-15; Rev 13:1-2; 17:11).

No 7-hill City mentioned in Scripture

The very popular and universal theory that Rome is the city of 7 hills of Rev 17 is truly unscriptural. In the first place, there is no mention of such a city in Rev 17 or in any other scripture. As seen above, the 7 heads on the beast of Rev 17 refer to kingdoms, not literal hills on which Rome, Moscow, or any other city is built. If the 7 heads referred to literal hills on which Rome is built we would have to believe and teach that 5 of these hills had already become flattened out before John wrote the Revelation, for "five are fallen" (Rev 17:10). Rome would be on only one hill at the time John wrote

Revelation, for only "one is" (Rev 17:10). And, Rome would have to be moved from this, the 6th hill, to a 7th hill sometime after he wrote Revelation, for only "one is not yet come" (Rev 17:12). From the 7th, which would continue "a short space" (Rev 17:10) Rome would be moved on to an 8th hill (Rev 17:11).

Such a theory is unreasonable but when we understand the 7 heads and the beast itself, as referring to 8 kingdoms, we do not have such a problem. These 8 kingdoms that have persecuted and will yet persecute Israel in "the times of the Gentiles" are Egypt, Assyria, Babylon, Medo-Persia, Greece, Rome, Revised Rome, and Revived Greece.

The beast of Rev 13 and 17 was "like a leopard," which in Dan 7:6 symbolized the old Grecian Empire. This is the one of the 5 kingdoms that had fallen before John wrote Revelation, and when it is revived again as predicted in Dan 7:7-8, 23-24; 8:7-9, 20-25 it will become the 8th kingdom of Rev 17:11. The 7th empire will be made up of 10 kingdoms, and the 8th will be the same 10 kingdoms only formed into one empire under the human Antichrist.

FALLACY 7: Antichrist is "the king of the north" and the king of Russia of Dan 11.

TRUTH: This fallacy is truly one of the most unscriptural. The popular theory that Russia will fulfill Ezek 38-39 and Dan 11:35-45, and that Russia will invade Israel in the near future before the battle of Armageddon, and before Antichrist reigns, is totally false. Instead of these two chapters being fulfilled with Russia invading Israel before the tribulation, they picture the Antichrist from Syria of the 10 kingdoms of the old Roman Empire invading Israel at the very end of the great tribulation which ends at the second coming of Christ to the earth to set up a kingdom. As we have seen, the 10 kingdoms must yet be formed "inside" the old Roman Empire area before Antichrist comes. Then, in his rise to power over them, he overthrows three of the 10 kingdoms (Dan 7:7-8, 23-24). This will bring us down to the middle of Daniel's 70th week and the time of the beginning of the reign of Antichrist over the 10 kingdoms for the last 3½ years of this age (Dan 7:7-8, 19-25; 8:7-25; 9:27; 11:40-45; Rev 17:8-17). At the beginning of his take over of the 10 kingdoms, 3½ years before the second advent of Christ, there will be a war declared on him and his 10 kingdoms by the countries of the north and east of the Roman Empire (Dan 11:44). He will then go forth against these new enemies and will conquer them in the last 3½ years that he reigns. He will be the "Gog" of Ezekiel 38-39, and will become the new ruler of Germany, Russia, China, Japan, India, and other parts of the north and east of his 10 kingdoms by conquest and not by originating in Russia, himself, or by coming from any one of these particular countries. As Gog, he will then bring all these nations down against Israel hoping to destroy the Jews, but will be defeated by Christ at His second advent in a one-day battle called Armageddon (Ezek 28-39; Isa 63; Joel 2-3; Zech 14; Mt 24:29-31; 2 Th 1:7-10; Jude 14-15; Rev 16:13-16; 19:11-21).

FALLACY 8: Antichrist will be a world-wide dictator and literally rule the whole earth. He will kill every man, woman, boy, and girl on earth who will not worship him as God, and who will not take his name, or his mark, or the number of his name in their right hand or in their forehead.

TRUTH: Not one of the above claims is true. Antichrist will never rule the whole earth; he will never be a world-wide dictator; he will never cause the whole world to worship him and his image, taking his name, the number of his name, or his mark — or be killed.

12 Proofs Antichrist will not Rule America or be a World-wide Dictator

Proof 1: The terms "all the world" and "the whole earth," and "all" must be understood in a figurative sense when used of a king or a kingdom of men. The figure of speech is *synecdoche* by which a part is put for the whole, or the whole for a part. It is used repeatedly in the Bible when only a part is meant. It is used by men daily in such language as "the whole country (state or city) was there last night," or "everybody in town was there." If we meant such a statement literally we would be telling a falsehood unless it could actually be proved.

In all the passages below we must keep in mind that the making of a law and the keeping of that law are two different things. Rev 13 does reveal that Antichrist will make a law that all in his 10 kingdoms must worship him and take his brands or be killed, but the execution of that law will be impossible to bring about for several reasons:

(1) Antichrist will only reign 3½ years after he makes the law of Rev 13:5, 16-18, and no human being could enforce such a law in such a short time throughout such a vast territory as the old Roman Empire. If he could not do so in this empire how could he do it — even if he ruled the whole world — throughout the entire earth, contacting every person of every continent and all the islands of the sea?

(2) He will be too busily occupied in wars with the nations north and east of the old Roman Empire territory to concentrate on enforcing such a law even within his own empire.

(3) He will be destroyed by Jesus Christ before he can literally enforce such a law throughout such a vast territory (Dan 7:11;

11:44-45; Rev 19:11-21; 2 Th 2:7-12).

Examples of a Part for a Whole
and a Whole for a Part:

(1) "I, even I, do bring a flood of waters upon the earth, to destroy *all flesh,* wherein is the breath of life, from under heaven; and *EVERY THING that is in the earth shall die*" (Gen 6:17). If we took this as literally as men do Rev 13, we would have Noah and his family and all the animals in the ark dead, for they were also under heaven and in the earth and yet they did not die.

(2) It is said of Nebuchadnezzar that God made him ruler over *"ALL men,"* but, as king of ancient Babylon he ruled over only a part of the earth (Dan 2:37, 38; 4:1, 11, 12, 20). He did not reign over Greece, Rome, and many other lands of that time. In Dan 2:39 Greece is spoken of as ruling over *"ALL the earth,"* but Greece did not reign over Italy, Spain, and many other countries at that time. In Dan 7:23, Rome is spoken of as ruling over the "whole earth," but we know that this did not include many tribes and nations on the earth. And so, *"all"* in these passages simply means that only a part of the earth was ruled by the king or kingdoms.

(3) In Mt 3:5, 6 we read, "Then went out to him Jerusalem, and *ALL Judea,* and *ALL the region* round about Jordan, and were baptized of him to Jordan, confessing their sins," but we know that the Pharisees, the Sadducees, and many others in all these parts were not baptized of John (Mt 21:25). Many women and children, the sick, and others of all classes never did see John, much less were baptized by him in Jordan. The truth intended is that many people from these parts were baptized by John.

(4) In Lk 2:1-3 we read that Caesar Augustus made a decree that *"ALL the world* should be taxed . . . .And *ALL* went to be taxed, every one to his own city." And, we know that any law made by a Roman emperor did not affect the many countries outside his own empire, so *"all"* here must be understood only in connection with the old Roman Empire that was under the rule of Caesar Augustus.

(5) In Rom 1:8 Paul said, "Your faith is spoken of throughout the *WHOLE world,"* but we know that he meant only that the local church at Rome was known by many in the various parts of the Roman Empire. Multitudes outside of Rome, and even many inside the Empire had never yet heard of the Christian faith, much less the local church at Rome. The same is true of Col 1:23 where we read that the gospel had been "preached to *EVERY CREATURE under heaven*"; and of Rom 10:18 where it is reported that it was preached "into *ALL the earth*" and "*UNTO THE ENDS OF THE WORLD.*" The gospel has not yet been taken to all nations, so we know the whole world was not evangelized in Paul's day.

With further reference to the word "all" let us understand the way it is used in each particular scripture. If it is used in an all inclusive sense it will be clear as in 1 Tim 2:4 where it is stated that God "will have *ALL* men to be saved, and to come unto the knowledge of the truth." This means all men without exception, for we find no other passage in the Bible to limit this, as in the case of a ruler reigning over a given territory — the case of Caesar Augustus over the Roman Empire, for instance, or the Antichrist over the 10 kingdoms.

Proof 2: In Rev 13:1 and 17:8-17 the beast is shown to have only 10 horns — not a hundred or so — and they are crowned. This reveals exactly how many kingdoms of the world will give their territory to the Antichrist for him to rule over during the last 3½ years of this age. The 10 horns are explained in Dan 7:23-24 as 10 kings and 10 kingdoms *inside* the old Roman Empire territory. The prediction is "out of this kingdom (from the inside of it, not from the outside of it also) are 10 kings that shall arise." Thus it is clear that Antichrist will reign only over the old Roman Empire territory and not over the whole world.

12 Facts about the 10 Toes and 10 Horns of Daniel and Revelation:

(1) The 10 toes make the complete Revised Roman Empire (Dan 2:38-45; 7:7-8, 19-24).

(2) Three will be overthrown by the little horn in his rise to power (Dan 7:8, 20, 24).

(3) The others of the 10 horns will surrender to the little horn (Rev 17:10-17).

(4) All will come from *inside* the Roman Empire territory (Dan 7:7, 20, 24).

(5) All will grow on the fourth head at the same time, not successively (Dan 7:7-8, 20).

(6) All will be on the head before the little horn grows (Dan 7:7-8, 20, 24).

(7) All will exist together and be succeeded by the kingdom of God (Dan 2:44-45; 7:9-14).

(8) All will rule along with the beast for 42 months (Dan 7:25; 12:1-7; Rev 17:8-17; 19:19-21).

(9) All will be conquered by the Lamb at the same battle of Armageddon (Rev 17:14; Dan 2:44).

(10) These, together with the beast, will destroy the whore (Rev 17:1-17).

(11) These will form the 8th and last Gentile kingdom (Rev 17:11).

(12) The 10 horns on the beast of Dan 7:7-8 are also upon the dragon of Rev 12:1-3 and the beast of Rev 13:1-3 — and they symbolize the same coming 10 kingdoms inside the Roman and Grecian empires.

Proof 3: In Rev 12:3 the dragon or Satan has only 10 horns — not dozens of them — and they are not crowned. This symbolizes that at that point in the middle of Daniel's 70th week he will give power over these 10 kingdoms to the Antichrist for 42 months or the last 3½ years of this age (Rev 13:1-5). It reveals that at the time Satan is cast our of heaven as in Rev 12:7-12 he has power only over these 10 kingdoms and not over all the nations of the entire earth. Another point proving this is the fact that he will have to do miracles before certain kings of the earth to get their co-operation at Armageddon (Rev 16:13-16). If they were already under Satan and directly controlled by him, and if they had no choice whatsoever as to whether they would follow him at Armageddon he would not need to seek their co-operation against Christ by performing the miracles mentioned in Rev 16:13-16.

Thus, again it is clear that the Antichrist will be limited to 10 kingdoms *inside* the old Roman Empire boundary instead of being a world-wide dictator ruling all other nations also outside the 10 kingdoms. His empire will be the same "all the world" that Caesar Augustus taxed in the day of his rule of the old Roman Empire (Lk 2:1-7). Antichrist will not rule any more of the world to begin with than Caesar Augustus did. And, it will be out of this same world that the 10 kingdoms will be formed in the last days (Dan 2:40-43; 7:7-8, 23-24; Rev 17:8-17).

Proof 4: In Rev 13:4 it is also revealed that there are to be nations outside the 10 kingdoms of Antichrist that are not under him. The questions asked are: "Who is like unto the beast? Who is able to make war on him?" This surely indicates nations outside the kingdom of Antichrist to compare him with and to question the making of war with him.

Proof 5: In Rev 13:7 and Dan 7:21-22 it is further revealed that there will be *saints* on the earth who will wage war against the Antichrist and many will be killed by him, but not all. This refers to saints *inside* the 10 kingdoms only, for it will be impossible for him to kill saints that are elsewhere in the many nations which are not a part of his 10-kingdom empire. The saints spoken of here are mainly the Jews who will flee from Judea and be protected by God the last 3½ years of this age. Jews by that time will have experienced their contract with Antichrist broken, and will become defeated in battle, being forced to flee out of Palestine (Dan 9:27; Mt 24:15-22; Rev 12:6, 14; Hos 2:14-18; Isa 16:1-6; Ezek 20:33-44; Ps 108:7-12).

The fact that not all the Jews are killed and they have a place elsewhere, reserved of God for 3½ years where He will protect them from both Antichrist and Satan proves that Antichrist will not be a world-wide dictator ruling all people and lands on the face of the earth (Rev 12:6, 14). At least 1/3 of the Jews of Palestine will be preserved alive through this ordeal (Zech 13:9; Rom 11:26). Multitudes of Jews in other lands will also be preserved from death at the hands of Antichrist and will be gathered alive to Palestine from all parts of the earth at the second advent (Isa 11:11-12; Mt 24:31). See full proof of this in fallacy 5, Chapter 9.

Proof 6: In Zech 14:16-21 it is revealed that many people of all nations, including many in the kingdom of the Antichrist, will not worship him and take his brands and be killed. They will live through the tribulation and continue into the Millennium and go up to Jerusalem year by year to worship Christ and pay homage to Him as their ruler. This passage shows that Egypt will be required to do this, and yet we read in Dan 11:40-43 that Egypt will not escape the Antichrist. She will be one of the 10 kingdoms. The passage makes it clear that some of all the nations who will be under Antichrist, as well as nations that are not under him, will at last live in the Millennium and go up to Jerusalem to worship Christ year after year. This proves that all men on earth will not worship the Antichrist and take his brands, and yet they will not be killed.

Proof 7: In Isa 66:19-21 it is stated that many heathen left on earth in the Millennium will finally hear about Christ and the gospel. But up to the end of the reign of Antichrist, at the second advent, they will not have heard of Christ nor seen His glory. If not by this time, then they also will not have heard of the Antichrist, the tribulation, and the reign of the beast. This proves that they will not have been in the kingdom of the Antichrist to know about his kingdom, his brands, and his worship. Had they heard about him, had worshipped him, and taken his brands they would have been executed and sent to eternal hell instead of being left alive on earth to worship Christ in the Millennium (Rev 14:9-11).

It is common knowledge that millions of heathen on earth today have never heard of Christ, or of the Antichrist. This will continue to be the case throughout the tribulation period and for some time on into the Millennium. They will hear of latter day events only after these events are over and Jewish missionaries go out from Jerusalem to tell the heathen that Christ is reigning in Zion (Isa 2:1-4; 52:7; 66:19-21; Zech 8:23; Mic 4:1-8).

If we contend that Antichrist will literally contact every man, woman, and child on earth in the 3½ years of the great tribulation we virtually say that this one human being will do more to contact the whole world than God, Christ, the Holy Spirit, angels, and redeemed men have done in about 2,000 years. All the heathen on earth have not been evangelized in all this time of the past and will not be so evangelized until sometime in the Millennium (Isa 2:1-4;

11:9; 52:7; Zech 8:23).

If it were true that Antichrist could accomplish such a feat as this: contact every human being on earth and kill off all who would not worship him and take his brands while, on the other hand God will, as predicted, send everyone to hell who does worship the Antichrist and take his brands, then there would not be one person left on earth for Christ to reign over when He comes to earth for that very purpose. That would leave the earth totally desolate. And that is not truth, for Christ will literally reign over all nations that are left on the earth — people who have escaped death during the tribulation (Isa 2:1-4; 9:6-7; Dan 2:44-45; 7:9-14, 18, 22, 27; Zech 14; Mt 24:29-31; 25:31-46; 2 Th 1:7-10; 2:7-8; Jude 14-15; Lk 1:32-33; Rev 11:15; 19:11-21; 20:1-10; 22:4-5).

Proof 8: In Dan 11:40-43 it is plainly stated that "many," not all nations of the earth, will be overthrown by Antichrist. And this is further proved by the fact that "many" nations will make war on him during the last 3½ years of this age when he is supposed to rule the whole world and force everybody to worship him. Dan 11:44 reveals that all the countries east and north of the 10 kingdoms will make war on Antichrist during this time. If they loved and worshipped him they would not be making war on him. They will, instead, be his enemies. Toward the end of these last 3½ years he will become victor over these new enemies and will then lead them against Jerusalem and the Jews at the second advent (Ezek 38-39; Zech 14; 2 Th 1:7-10; Jude 14-15; Rev 16:13-16; 19:11-21). Christ will be the victor in this battle of Armageddon and will then set up His kingdom in the world (Mt 25:31-46; Rev 11:15).

Proof 9: Not only is it revealed that Antichrist's kingdom will be limited to the old Roman Empire territory during the last 3½ years of this age, and that this will be the only part of the earth ruled by him, but it is also stated that certain parts of the earth, next to the Roman Empire territory itself, will "escape out of his hands." Three ancient Bible nations that make up modern Jordan are predicted to escape the Antichrist — they will not be ruled by him during this whole time that numerous scholars say he will be accepted and worshipped by all the world as God. Dan 11:41 says, "These shall escape out of his hands, even Edom, and Moab, and chief of the children of Ammon." Thus Jordan, which borders the Antichrist's kingdom, will escape him and not be ruled by him.

Israel in Judea will also escape Antichrist during all of the last 3½ years of this age. Their land will not escape, but the nation itself will do so by fleeing into Jordan, a country that will escape Antichrist. This is what Jesus meant when He said, "let them which be in Judea flee into the mountains . . . For then shall be great tribulation" such as never was or ever will be again (Mt 24:15-22). Isaiah 16:1-5 predicts the same thing saying, "Let mine outcasts dwell in thee, Moab." This prophecy commands Moab to protect Israel and not to betray them during this time. It even predicts that Israel will be welcomed by the Moabites at that time of the flight from the Antichrist. Ezek 20:33-44 also predicts the flight of Israel into Jordan when God will send the two witnesses of Rev 11:3-12 to do miracles and protect Israel as Moses and Aaron did in the wilderness in the days of their coming out of Egypt. They will bring Israel back to God during this great tribulation (Zech 4:14; Mal 4:5-6). And, Hosea 2:14-18 predicts the same event — that Israel will go into the wilderness in the end time and that, at this time, God will again marry Israel and make her an eternal nation under Christ.

Lastly, we have Israel, the woman of Rev 12, fleeing into the wilderness where she has a place prepared by God to feed and protect her during the time of her flight from Antichrist (Rev 12:1-17). Israel will be miraculously protected by God through the many miracles of the two witnesses, even to the extent of the earth literally opening up and swallowing the first armies of Satan and Antichrist so that she will get safely into her place of protection prepared for her by God (Rev 12:13-17). All this will take place after the 144,000 (all the saved or born again men of Israel) will have been raptured to heaven (Rev 7:1-8; 9:4; 12:5; 14:1-5). Thus, Jordan, and Israel who will flee into the wilderness of Jordan, will escape the Antichrist who will be ruling in Jerusalem at that time (Mt 24:15-22; 2 Th 2:1-4; Rev 11:1-2; Dan 9:27). In view of this it certainly is understandable that many other countries far across the oceans can and will escape Antichrist and not be ruled by him. If he cannot enforce his will upon people in a border country, it is truly understandable that he will not be able to accomplish this regarding other countries so far away.

Proof 10: In Mt. 13:39-49; 25:31-46 we have proof that there will be "righteous," and "just," and "good" people — "brethren" and "sheep" nations that have lived through the tribulation who will be permitted to enter into the eternal kingdom. If they had taken the brands of Antichrist and worshiped him they would be sent to hell at this judgment of the nations, for all who do this will not be permitted to live any longer on the earth after the second advent (Rev 14:9-11). Some of the people or nations will not be a part of the kingdom of Antichrist and will escape because of this, while others in the kingdom of the Antichrist will escape because the wars in the north and east will make it impossible to enforce such a law literally, as marking and killing many millions of people in such a vast empire as that of the Antichrist in such a short time as 42 months (Rev 13:5).

Proof 11: The fact that the "elect" of Israel will not be fully gathered from all nations until the second advent (Mt 24:29-31) proves that there will be a great many living in various nations and parts of the earth where Antichrist has not ruled and therefore has had no power to kill them because of not taking his brands, etc. These will escape Antichrist and the great tribulation on Israel in Judea, and will remain alive to be gathered after the tribulation that will be felt mainly in the 10 kingdoms. See the 70 great sections of Scripture in Chapter 9, fallacy 5, that prove such a gathering of "all Israel" at the second coming of Christ. One thing is certain: if Antichrist would have the power and authority over *all* nations in the tribulation period he would never permit all these thousands and millions of Jews to escape him.

Proof 12: In Rev 16:13-16 we have proof that the Antichrist will not be the ruler of the entire earth during the last 3½ years of this age, for at that same time, many nations will not yet be conquered and controlled by him. For this very reason, unclean spirits like frogs will go forth from the mouths of the Devil, the Antichrist, and the False Prophet to do miracles, seeking the cooperation and help of such nations at Armageddon. If these three controlled these nations and if the people of the nations loved Antichrist enough to worship him and Satan, they would not have to be prodded, stirred up, and urged to help out in the effort to defeat Jesus Christ in the coming battle of Armageddon. How many people of the various nations will cooperate with this satanic trinity is not stated, but no doubt some will gladly cooperate hoping to keep control of the planet earth and prevent Christ from setting up His kingdom. At any rate, this scripture is sufficient to prove that all nations of the earth will not be controlled by Antichrist at any point from the time of his rise to the time he is destroyed by Christ at Armageddon. He is to be defeated and personally killed by Christ at Jerusalem before he conquers even Israel and Jordan, and so, crossing the oceans to conquer nations who have not been under him, is something that could not happen. We must therefore conclude that ANTICHRIST WILL NOT BE A WORLD WIDE DICTATOR and HE WILL NEVER HAVE A WORLD GOVERNMENT even for one day of his whole career on earth to fulfill the prophecies uttered about him.

See the Map on page 118 showing the FULL EXTENT OF ANTI-CHRIST'S KINGDOM.

Chapter 5

12 Proofs Ezek 38-39 will not be fulfilled in a War between Russia and Israel:

There are four great prophecies that we must understand along with the predictions of Daniel before we can fully comprehend latter day events as they relate to the many scriptures on the rapture and the second advent. They are: Ezek 38-39; Mt 24-25; 2 Th 2; and the book of Revelation. The last two sections will be fully dealth with in Chapter 10, below, which see. The first two will be dealt with here and in the following order — Ezek 38-39, and then Mt 24-25.

Ezek 38-39 is generally interpreted as referring to a war between Russia and Israel sometime before the future tribulation and before the battle of Armageddon which takes place at the second advent of Christ. But the truth is that this whole prophecy will be fulfilled at Armageddon. No war, as described in these chapters, will be fought between Russia or any other country, and Israel until the time of the second coming of Christ, and then it will be a one day battle between Christ and Antichrist. It will also fulfill Isa 63:1-5; 64:1-5; Joel 2-3; Zech 14; Mt 24:29-31; 2 Th 1:7-10; Jude 14-15; Rev 14:14-20; 16:13-16; 19:11-21. *Note the following proofs:*

Proof 1: The fact that Russia is not mentioned in particular in Ezek 38-39 should be proof enough that Russia is not the subject of these chapters. The only reference to Russia in all Bible prophecy is in Dan 11:44 where she is included with other nations who are in the north and east of the old Roman Empire, but she is not mentioned by name in this verse or any other verse of the Bible. Dan 11:44 predicts that Antichrist, the king of the north, the king of Syria, will go forth to utterly destroy many countries of the north and east of his 10-kingdom empire. And, Russia is defintely situated north of both Syria and the 10 kingdoms to be under Antichrist at that time. Regarding the whole of Ezek 38-39 these chapters picture Antichrist, after having conquered the countries of the north and east, bringing all these newly conquered nations with him against Christ in an effort to stop Him from setting up His earthly kingdom. They picture an invasion of Israel by many nations — and this will never be until the time of the second advent at the end of the tribulation (Zech 14: Rev 19:11-21).

Proof 2: To say, as in the popular theory, that Russia is "the king of the north" spoken of in Dan 11:40-45 because she is the farthest north of any of the nations, does not prove the point. If so, then where are the countries still north of Russia, the so-called king of the north, which are predicted in this passage to make war on that particular "king of the north" or Russia? Thus, we see the impossibility of Russia's being the one referred to in Dan 11:40-45. We must look for such a king elsewhere — one that can fulfill this prophecy by being south of Russia and still north of Israel. The answer is found in Syria — not Russia. For Syria definitely relates to Israel as being in the north, and Russia is still further north — in a position north of Syria to wage war with "the king of the north" or Syria in the end time.

Proof 3: There are three main facts that prove that Gog of Ezek 38-39, who is the "little horn" of Dan 7:7-8, 23-24; 8:7-8, 20-23, and "the beast" of Rev 13-19, does not originate in Russia, but becomes the leader of Russia and all the countries in the north and east by conquest.

(1) He comes from the Roman Empire territory *after* the 10 kingdoms are formed *inside* that empire (Dan 7:7-8, 23-24; 8:7-9, 20-23).

(2) He comes from one of the 4 divisions of the old Grecian Empire, which will become 4 kingdoms of the 10 kingdoms of Dan 7 (Dan 8:7-9, 20-23).

(3) He conquers the countries north and east of the Roman Empire territory, but originates from Syria (Dan 11:36-45). He, therefore, becomes the scourge of Russia and not her hero and chief son.

Proof 4: At least 38 predictions in Ezekiel identify these chapters as being fulfilled at Armageddon at the second advent, and not at the time of some hypothetical war between Israel and Russia happening before the tribulation and the second advent. The predictions include: both Israel and many other nations getting to know God from the time of this battle onward (38:16; 39:6-7, 21-25, 27); no more pollution of God's name (39:7); God glorified by all nations (39:13, 21); Israel saved from Gentile domination forever (39:26-29); Israel completely regathered from all nations (39:28); the Holy Spirit poured out upon Israel (39:29); Israel never again to be afraid of other nations (39:26); God never again to hide His face from Israel (39:29); God's name to be sanctified among the heathen (39:7); men to see God bodily and in person (38:18-22; 39:1-6, 17-24); and all the heathen to know God from this time forward into all ternity (39:23; Rev 21-22).

These predictions could not be fulfilled before the end of the tribulation and the second advent (Zech 14; Mt 24:29-21; 25:31-46; 2 Th 1:7-10; Jude 14-15; Rev 19:11-21. See also many similar statements in Ezek 16:62; 17:24; 20:38-44; 30:8, 19, 25-26;

34:27-30; 35:9; 36:11-36; 37:6-28). The predictions relate therefore to Armageddon and not to a war between Russia and Israel before Antichrist conquers the many countries in the north and east, forcing the Russians and other nations to cooperate with him at Armageddon (Ezek 38-39; Zech 14; Rev 16:1-16; 19:11-21).

Proof 5: Gog and his armies of Ezek 38-39 falling upon the open field to make a great supper for the birds and beasts is exactly the same as in Rev 14:12-20; 19:11-21; Mt 24:28, 37-42; Lk 17:34-37 which pictures the battle of Armageddon (Ezek 38:3-5; 39:4, 17-25).

Proof 6: God predicts that the armies of Gog in Ezek 38:20-22; 39-6 would become so confused that they would destroy one another. The same is stated of the armies of the Antichrist at Armageddon (Zech 14:4, 10).

Proof 7: Ezek 38-39 predicts and describes something more than an ordinary war between two earthly nations only, such as Russia and Israel. The passage describes a battle that is mainly a supernatural war between Satan, his angels and demons, with Antichrist and his earthly armies on one side, and Jesus Christ, His angels, the resurrected saints, and Israel on the other side. Supernatural and miraculous things will be happening on both sides, as is clear in Zech 14; Joel 2-3; Mt 16:27; 24:29-31; 25:31-46; 2 Th 1:7-10; 2:7-12; Jude 14-15; Rev 16:13-21; 19:11-21. It will be the last war on earth before the Millennium, the real Armageddon – the fourth and last of 4 great wars between now and then.

4 Great Wars between now and the Millennium:

(1) The war to form the 10 kingdoms out of about 25 governments that are now *inside* the old Roman Empire territory (Dan 7:7-8, 19-25; Rev 17:8-17). This will happen *before* Daniel's 70th week and *before* the future tribulation and reign of Antichrist.

(2) The war causing Antichrist from Syria to overthrow 3 of the 10 kingdoms which will cause the other six to surrender to him without any further battle (Dan 7:7-8, 19-25; 8:7-14, 20-23; 11:40-45; Rev 17:8-17). This war will last for 3½ years or during the first half of Daniel's 70th week, after which Antichrist will be given power over the whole 10 kingdoms for 42 months (Dan 7:7-8, 19-25; 12:7; Rev 13:5; 17:8-17).

(3) The war between Antichrist and the countries north and east of his 10 kingdoms (Dan 11:44). This will be during the last 3½ years of Daniel's 70th week, and will include time for the mobilization of the nations for Armageddon where they hope to stop Christ from landing on the planet earth, and also plan to annihilate Israel (Zech 14:1-15; Rev 16:13-21; 19:11-21).

(4) The Battle of Armageddon itself, which will be only one day long – the day Christ lands on the mount of Olives to defeat and to destroy the vast armies of the nations that will be under Gog (Ezek 38-39; Isa 63:1-5; 64:1-5; Joel 2-3; Zech 14; Mt 24:29-31; 2 Th 1:7-10; 2:8-12; Jude 14-15; Rev 16:13-21, 19:11-21).

Proof 8: There are to be two invasions of Israel by Gog, the Antichrist from the Syria section of the Roman and Grecian Empires; and so, it is not Russia that will fulfill the scriptures of both Daniel and Revelation.

Two future Invasions of Israel by the Antichrist:

(1) The first invasion of Israel by the Antichrist is to be in the middle of Daniel's 70th week when he breaks his 7-year covenant with Israel (Dan 9:27; 11:40-43; Mt 24:15-22; Rev 12:1-17). At this point he suddenly defeats Israel, taking over their city and temple, and declares himself to be God (Dan 7:21-22, 25; Mt 24:15-22; 2 Th 2:1-4; Rev 11:1-2; 12:1-17). Israel flees into the wilderness of Jordan where she is to be protected by God from the Antichrist for 3½ years (Isa 16:1-5; Ps 108; Mt 24:15-22; Ezek 20:33-44; Hos 2:14-18; Rev 11:1-2). The two witnesses appear on earth to lead and protect Israel by miraculous powers (Rev 11:2-12; Mal 4:5-6; Zech 4:14). An army of the Antichrist fighting Israel at that time will literally be swallowed up by the earth (Rev 12:6-17). And then, at that point the combined nations of the north and east will make war on Antichrist (Dan 11:44) who will break off his main effort to follow Israel into the wilderness, planning to come back against Israel after he conquers the armies of the north and east, which he does in less than 3½ years, thus fulfilling Ezek 38-39 in time to meet Christ in battle at the second advent (Zech 14; Rev 19:19-21). This is how God shortens the great tribulation of Israel in the last 3½ years (Mt 24:22). It is the intensity of the great tribulation that God cuts short, not the length of the 3½ years of the period, itself.

(2) The second invasion of Israel by Gog, or the Antichrist, will be at the end of the great tribulation after he has conquered the countries of the north and east during the 42 months of his reign (Dan 11:44; Rev 13:5). During this time (toward the end of this tribulation) Israel, by the help of God and the two witnesses, will regain possession of Jerusalem. Then Gog (Antichrist) will come down from the north and east with his vast armies to retake Jerusalem and hope to annihilate Israel. He will regain Jerusalem and take half of the city captive (Zech 14:1-9). Then suddenly Christ will appear from heaven with all His raptured saints and His angels, and will defeat Antichrist and all his armies in one day of battle –

Armageddon. Christ will proceed to set up the judgment of the nations and also regather Israel from all the earth (Mt 24:29-31; 25:31-46; Isa 11:11-12; Zech 14; Ezek 38-39; 2 Th 1:7-10; 2:8-12; Jude 14-15; Rev 16:13-21; 19:11-21).

Proof 9: The complete regathering of Israel, God's elect, from all nations after the battle of Ezek 38-39 proves that these two chapters refer in detail to the battle of Armageddon at the second advent, and not to some pre-tribulation invasion of Israel by Russia. God says He will restore them to their original land of promise (Ezek 39:25-29). Restoring the captivity of Israel here is the same as that in Isa 11:11-12 and many other passages, as we quote in fallacy 5, Chapter 9, below. After this regathering Israel will dwell safe in her own land (Ezek 39:26). If Ezek 38-39 became fulfilled in a war between Russia and Israel years before Armageddon then why would Israel have to go through the greatest of all tribulations during the last 3½ years of this age? Why would she have to wait until Armageddon was over before dwelling safe in her own land?

Proof 10: Gog and his armies cannot be destroyed in Palestine while they are away fighting in the north and east, fulfilling Dan 11:44, and not before they conquer the north and east and lead the vast armies down against Jerusalem to fight at Armageddon. There being only one destruction of Gentile armies in Palestine predicted in Ezek 38:18-22; 39:1-7, 17-20, and Armageddon being the only time of total destruction of the Gentile world armies, then Ezek 38-39 and Armageddon must refer to the same battle at the second advent of Christ.

Proof 11: We have no authority for bringing Russia into the picture as the fulfillment of Ezek 38-39 because the word "rosh" is used in these two chapters (Ezek 38:2-3; 3:1). Actually, the word *Russia* is not derived from *rosh,* as some teach seeking to force Russia into prophecy. The Encyclopedia Britannica says that the *Rus* were a tribe related to the Swedes, Angles, and Northmen. They are referred to as *Rus* by Arabian writers as well as by the Byzantine writers who also refer to the Russians as *Rus,* but never as *rosh.*

The Heb. word *rosh* never means *Russia* either inside or outside the Bible. In the King James Version it is translated *chief* in Ezek 38:2-3; 19:1. Besides being used in these scriptures *rosh* is used in the Heb. Bible 590 times and in 20 different ways, as follows: *chief* 100 times; *chiefest* 1 time; *company* 5 times; *excellent* 1 time; *first* 7 times; *forefront* 1 time; *height* 1 time; *high* 2 times; *lead* 1 time; *principal* 5 times; *rulers* 2 times; *sum* 10 times; *top* 67 times; *head* 270 times; *heads* 90 times; *bands* 2 times; *beginning* 11 times; *captain* 4 times; *captains* 6 times; and *chapiters* 4 times. It is not translated Russia one time.

Proof 12: It is sometimes argued that Russia is the fulfillment of these chapters because of the mention of the tribes of Meshech and Tubal, and of the land of Magog — sons of Noah through Japheth (Gen 10:1-5). But we cannot say that all the ancient descendants of these tribes of Noah were Russians, for there were many peoples of Europe and Asia who came from the sons of Noah. Josephus, who lived 37-96 A.D. and who wrote a history covering the period from Adam to his own death in 96 A.D. said that Magog's sons were called Sythians and they settled around the Black Sea. He said also that the sons of Japheth settled in the Taurus mountains of Asia Minor, and then spread to many other lands. He said furthermore that from Gomer came the Galatians; from Madai came the Medes; from Javan came the Greeks; from Tubal and Meshech came the ancient Iberians and Cappadocians of Asia Minor, or modern Turkey; and from Tiras came the Thracians. It was from these ancient peoples that all of Asia and Europe were inhabited, not Russia alone.

Chapter 6

Exposition of Mt 24-25

These two chapters, next to Ezek 38-39, must be truly understood if we want all the questions concerning the rapture and the second advent to be cleared up. Most of the fallacies of men regarding these two subjects come from a wrong understanding of prophecy, and because we do not take literally what we read in prophecy. As a whole we are leaning to the mystical, spiritual, symbolic and figurative – even to the sensational instead of turning to that which is literal and simple to understand. To begin with, the church is not once mentioned in Mt 24-25, much less the rapture of the church. As long as we allow the church and its rapture to be injected into these chapters which deal absolutely and exclusively with Israel and the second coming of Christ to set up a kingdom in the world, then we shall be confused. Some men today are rejecting the rapture altogether because they struggle to find the church in these two chapters and it is simply not there. If we would regard the Bible even half as sensibly as we do other writings, we would not have such confusion. If any other book said plainly that its subject was ISRAEL and made no mention of the church we would more than likely read the book from that standpoint. If we sought to force the church into the book that was written exclusively for Jews we could not help becoming confused. So it is with Mt 24-25. This is one discourse wherein we must keep the church out of it, if we want the truth.

3 Questions asked of Jesus by His Jewish disciples:

1. *"Tell us when shall these things be?"* Jesus had just announced that the time was coming when there would not be one stone of the Jewish temple at Jerusalem which would not be thrown down (Mt 24:2). He did not predict that St. Peter's church in Rome or any other church building at any other place in the world would be thrown down. He simply limited His prediction to the one temple – the temple of Herod at Jerusalem, saying it would be thrown down. And, we know from history that Christ referred to the destruction of the temple by the Romans in 70 A.D., when His prophecy was fulfilled. Luke tells us that "when ye shall see Jerusalem compassed with armies, then know that the the desolation thereof is nigh" (Lk 21:20-24). And, Luke further explains that when Jerusalem would be destroyed (as in 70 A.D.) the Jews, themselves, would fall by the

edge of the sword and many be led away captive among all nations until the time of the Gentiles would be fulfilled. Jerusalem was also to be trodden down of the Gentiles until the times of the Gentiles would be fulfilled. In answering the above question Jesus was therefore talking to national Israel, and not the church.

Only in our generation have the Jews begun to go back to Palestine and are now building up a great nation in fulfillment of Ezek 37 and many other scriptures. See Chapter 9, fallacy 5. Not many years ago Jerusalem was still in Gentile hands, and those of us who knew the Bible said that the Jews would have to be given control of the city again to fulfill prophecy. We based our conclusion upon the fact that the city would have to be in Jewish control in order to be given back to the Gentiles, as predicted, for the last 42 months of this age (Rev 11:1-2). Now we are saying that no man or combination of men and nations will defeat Israel enough to take the city from them again UNTIL in the days of Antichrist when he breaks his covenant with Israel in the middle of Daniel's 70th week (Dan 9:27; Mt 24:15-22; Rev 11:1-2). At that time Israel will be defeated by the Gentiles and have to flee into the wilderness (Dan 11:40-43; Isa 16:1-5; Ezek 20:33-44; Hos 2:14-18; Mt 24:16; Rev 12:6, 14). The Jews will then get control of the city again at the end of the tribulation but Antichrist, when he comes down with his armies from the north and east, will take the city once again (Zech 14:1-5).

2. *The second question* asked by His Jewish disciples was, "What shall be the sign of thy coming?" This was plainly a question asking for some signs or evidences whereby they might know of the nearness of His coming to the earth again.

The coming that the disciples asked about could not have been the rapture of the church to heaven, but rather the literal, visible, second advent that will end this age. Christ had told them many times about His visible coming to the earth to set up a kingdom, such as in Mt 13:30-50; 16:27; 23:37-39. Whenever Christ mentioned His second advent, His disciples knew full well that He was talking about His coming to the earth to set up His kingdom over Israel, and not over the church (Gen 49:10; Isa 9:6-7; Jer 30:31; Ezek 37; 43:7; Dan 2:44-45; 7:9-14, 18, 22, 27; Hos 3:4-5; Zech 14; Mt. 16:27; 24:29-31; 25:31-46). This concern for the establishment of the Jewish kingdom on earth was uppermost in their minds. The last question they asked Him some 40 days later when He was about to ascend to heaven was: "Lord, wilt thou at this time restore again the kingdom to Israel?" (Acts 1:6-7). Their questions were about the political and literal kingdom of Israel, not about the N. T. church. A summary of the events to take place between the rapture and the second advent will be helpful at this point.

100 Prophetical Events between the Rapture and the Second Advent

We shall divide the 100 signs or prophetic events of the latter days into 5 sections of Daniel's 70th week, that is, the whole 7 years of tribulation and the reign of Antichrist which will take place between the time of the rapture of the church and O. T. saints, and the second advent, as follows:

I. *Events that will begin the 70th week:*

1. A 7-year covenant between Israel and Antichrist (Dan 9:27)
2. Rise of the Antichrist from Syria in an attempt to conquer the whole world (Dan 7:7-8, 23-24; 8:7-14, 20-23; 11:40-45; Rev 6:1-8).

II. *Events that will happen during the first 3½ years of the Week:*

3. Beginning of Israel's travail, including deceptions, wars, rumors of war, famines, pestilences, earthquakes (Mt 24:1-8; Mk 13:7-8; Lk 21:8-10; Rev 6:1-8).
4. THEN Gentiles will deliver Israel up to be destroyed (Mt 24:9; Mk 13:9)
5. Many offenses and betrayals of Israel (Mt 24:9-10; Mk 13:9)
6. Many false prophets doing miracles (Mt 24:11, 24; Rev 13:11-18; 16:13-20)
7. Sin and iniquity abounding (Mt 24:12; 1 Tim 4: 2 Tim 3-4; Jude 14-19; Rev 9:20-21)
8. Love of many waxing cold (Mt 24:12)
9. Gospel as a witness to all nations (Mt 24:14; Mk 13:10)
10. Fearful sights among men (Lk 21:11)
11. Great signs in the heavens (Lk 21:11)
12. Signs in the sun, moon, and stars (Lk 21:25)
13. Distress and perplexity of nations (Lk 21:25)
14. Seas and waves roaring – tidal waves (Lk 21:25)
15. Men's hearts failing them for fear (Lk 21:26)
16. Great shaking in the heavens (Lk 21:26)
17. Great hope for Israel (Lk 21:28)
18. Martyrdom of saints by the great whore (Rev 17:6)
19. Settlement of raptured saints in their mansions in heaven (Jn 14:1-3; Heb 11:10-16; 12:22-23; 13:14)
20. Concert in heaven by the raptured church and O. T. saints (Rev 5:8-10)
21. All creations worship God (Rev 4:4-11; 5:5-14)
22. Opening of the first seal – rise of Antichrist (Rev 6:1-2; Dan 7:7-8, 23-24; 8:8-15, 20-23; 11:40-45)

23. Opening of the second seal — war (Rev 6:3-4; Dan 7:7-8, 23-24; 11:40-45)

24. Opening of the third seal — famine (Rev 6:5-6; Mt 24:4-8; Lk 21:8-11)

25. Opening of the fourth seal — death and hell loosed (Rev 6:7-8)

26. Opening of the fifth seal — martyrdom of saints (Rev 6:9-11; 17:6).

27. Opening of the sixth seal — great changes in the earth, moon, stars, and sun — wrath of God begins (Rev 6:12-17; Lk 21:11, 25-33)

28. Sealing of the 144,000 Jews for protection from the trumpet judgments (Rev 7:1-8; 9:4; 12:5; 14:1-5)

29. Great revival — multitudes saved and martyred (Rev 6:9-11; 7:9-17; Acts 2:16-21)

30. Opening of the seventh seal — silence in heaven (Rev 8:1)

31. Seven angels prepare to blow trumpets (Rev 8:2-6)

32. The first trumpet — hail, fire, and blood rained upon the earth (Rev 8:7)

33. The second trumpet — sea to blood (Rev 8:8-9)

34. The third trumpet — waters poisoned (Rev 8:10-11)

35. The fourth trumpet — sun, moon, stars darkened (Rev 8:12)

36. Announcement of three great woes on men (Rev 8:13)

37. The fifth trumpet — torment by demons for 5 months (Rev 9:1-11)

38. The sixth trumpet — 200,000,000 demons kill one-third of men (Rev 9:12-21)

39. A great angel appears on earth (Rev 10:1-11)

40. Destruction of the great whore by Antichrist and his 10 kings (Rev 17:7-17)

III. *Events that will happen in the middle of Daniel's 70th week:*

41. Antichrist breaks his 7-year covenant with Israel and declares war (Dan 9:27)

42. The abomination of desolation — Jewish sacrifices suspended, Antichrist and his image worshipped in the Jewish temple (Dan 9:27; Mt 24:15; Rev 13:11-18)

43. Sudden defeat of Israel by Antichrist (Dan 8:24; 11:40-43)

44. Jerusalem conquered by Antichrist (Rev 11:1-2; 2 Th 2:1-4)

45. Jewish temple, built sometime before this, now made the capital building of Antichrist (Dan 8:9-14; 9:27; Mt 24:15-22; 2 Th 2:1-4; Rev 13:11-18)

46. Israel, defeated by Antichrist, flees into Jordan (Dan 11:40-43; Isa 16:1-5; Ezek 20:33-34; Ps 108; Hos 2:14-18; Mt 24:15-22; Rev 12:6, 14)

47. The **great tribulation** begins (Rev 11:1-2; 12:6, 14; Isa 66:7-8; Jer. 30:7; Dan 12:1; Mt 24:15-22).

48. Defeat of Egypt, Turkey, and Greece by the Antichrist (Dan 7:7-8, 23-24; 11:40-43)

49. The whole 10 kingdoms surrender to Antichrist for 42 months (Dan 7:7-8, 23-24; 11:40-43; Rev 13:5; 17:8-17)

50. Formation of the 10 kingdoms into one empire — the eighth kingdom, or the old Grecian Empire revived (Dan 7:23-24; 8:7-15, 20-23; 11:40-43; Rev 17:8-17)

51. Rise of the false prophet with satanic powers (Rev 13:11-18; 16:13-16)

52. Antichrist endued with satanic power (Dan 11:35-39; 2 Th 2:7-12; Rev 13:2; 16:13-16)

53. The seventh trumpet — the third woe on man — casting out of Satan and his angels for 3½ years (Rev 8:13; 9:12; 10:5-7; 11:14; 12:7-12)

54. The two witnesses appear on earth for 3½ years (Rev 11:1-12; Mal 4:5-6; Zech 4:14; Ezek 20:33-34; Hos 2:14-18; Isa 16:1-5)

55. Sun-clothed woman delivered of a manchild (Rev 12:1-5; Isa 66:7-8; Dan 12:1)

56. Rapture of the manchild — the 144,000 — to heaven (Rev 7:1-8; 9:4; 12:5; 14:1-4; Isa 66:7-8; Dan 12:1). See Chapters 10-11 below.

IV. *Events of the last 3½ years of Daniel's 70th week:*

57. Establishment of the new religion of worship of Antichrist and his image (Rev 13:11-18; 14:9-11; 15:1-4; 20:4-6)

58. Branding of men who follow Antichrist (Rev 13:16-18; 14:9-11; 15:1-4; 20:4-6)

59. Martyrdom of saints in the old Roman Empire territory by Antichrist (Dan 7:21-25; 8:9-14, 24; 12:1; Isa 66:7-8; Jer 30:7; Mt 24:15-22; Rev 7:9-17; 11:7; 13:7-18; 14:9-11; 15:1-4; 20:4-6)

60. Great blasphemies against God by Antichrist (Dan 7:25; Rev 13:6)

61. Changing of laws by Antichrist (Dan 7:25; Rev 13:16-18).

62. Invasion and defeat of the nations north and east of the Antichrist and his 10 kingdoms (Dan 11:44)

63. Many Jewish conversions from God to Antichrist (Jn 5:43; Dan 8:10-12, 21-24; 11:45)

64. Great deceptions accomplished by Antichrist (Dan 8:24-25; 2 Th 2:7-12; Rev 12:9)

65. Antichrist's destruction of 2/3 of Israel (Zech 13:9; Mt 24:15-20; Dan 7:21-24; 8:24-25; Rev 12:5, 14)

66. Death and rapture to heaven of the two witnesses (Rev 11:3-12)

67. Temple of God opened in heaven (Rev. 11:19)

68. Announcement of the third woe on men (Rev 8:13; 9:12; 10:4-7; 11:14; 12:7-12)

69. An army of Satan and Antichrist swallowed up by the earth (Rev 12:13-17)

70. War on the remnant of Israel in Palestine (Rev 12:13-17)

71. Concert in heaven by the 144,000 Jews (Rev 14:1-5)

72. First of three messenger angels appears – everlasting gospel preached (Rev 14:6-7)

73. Second messenger angel announces fall of Babylon (Rev 14:8)

74. Third messenger angel announces doom of beast worshippers (Rev 14:9-11)

75. Annnouncement of blessings upon those who are martyred from henceforth (Rev 14:12-13)

76. Announcement of Armageddon being like a harvest (Rev 14:14-16)

77. Announcement of Armageddon being like a vintage (Rev 14:17-20)

78. Seven vial judgment angels prepare to pour out the wrath of God (Rev 16:1)

79. Concert in heaven by the tribulation martyrs (Rev. 15:1-4; 20:4-6)

80. Temple of God in heaven opened again (Rev 15:5-8. Cp. Rev 11:18)

81. Special announcement to the 7 vial angels (Rev 16:1)

82. The first vial – ulcers upon beast-marked men (Rev 16:2)

83. The second vial – sea turned to blood (Rev 16:3)

84. The third vial – rivers to blood (Rev 16:4-7)

85. The fourth vial – men scorched with fire of the sun (Rev 16:8-9)

86. The fifth vial – darkness upon the kingdom of Antichrist (Rev 16:10-11)

87. The sixth vial – river Euphrates dried up (Rev 16:12)

88. Demons with miraculous powers gathering the nations to Armageddon (Rev 16:13-16)

89. The seventh vial – great hail and earthquakes (Rev 16:17-21; 18:1-24; Ezek 38:20; Zech 14:4)

90. Appearance of the redeemed before the judgment seat of Christ in heaven (1 Cor 3:11-15; 2 Cor 5:10; Rom 14:10)

91. Marriage Supper of the Lamb in heaven (Rev 19:1-10)

V. *Events that will end Daniel's 70th week:*

92. Second advent of Christ and termination of the great tribulation (Rev 19:11-12; Jude 14-15; Zech 14:1-5; 2 Th 1:7-10; 2:7-12; Mt 24:29-31; Isa 63)

93. Battle of Armageddon on the first day of the second advent (Ezek 38-39; Isa 63; Zech 14:1-15; Mt 24:29-31; 2 Th 1:7-10; 2:7-8; Jude 14-15; Rev 16:13-16; 19:11-21)

94. Conversion of the nation of Israel to God in one day (Isa 66:7-8; Zech 12:10-13:1; Mt 23:37-39; Rom 11:25-29)

95. All transgression of Israel finished (Dan 9:24)

96. An end to all sins in Israel (Dan 9:24)

97. Full reconciliation of Israel to God (Dan 9:24)

98. Bringing in everlasting righteousness for Israel (Dan 9:24)

99. Completion of visions and many prophecies concerning Israel and Jerusalem (Dan 9:24)

100. Anointing of the most holy (Dan 9:24)

5 Reasons the Rapture of the Church takes place before the above Events:

(1) Christ promised that all worthy ones who qualify for heaven would "escape all these things" and "stand before the Son of man" (Lk 21:34-36)

(2) Christ confirmed this truth — the escape of every believer who would qualify for heaven at the time of the rapture — by showing that every detail of the book of Revelation, from Rev 4:1 through the rest of the book, would be fulfilled "AFTER THE CHURCH" is raptured (Rev 1:19, 4:1). See full proof of this in Chapter 10, proof 2, below.

(3) Paul plainly told the Thessalonians that Antichrist must come *before* the day of the Lord (2 Th 1:2-3), and the church would be raptured *before* Antichrist would come (2 Th 2:7-8). See Chapter 10, proof 1, below.

(4) Paul further confirmed this when, in speaking of the coming of the day of the Lord, he said that "God hath not appointed us to wrath" — wrath of the seals, trumpets, and vials which is to take place at that particular time (1 Th 5:1-11)

(5) No less than four times in the book of Revelation, John records that raptured saints are in heaven singing, having concerts and eating food, while the events of Rev 4:1-19:21 are taking place. In Rev 5:8-10 the church and O. T. saints are seen in heaven at the time John begins to write about the things which must be AFTER THE CHURCH age. Next in the fulfillment of these things, which must be after the rapture, John records that the 144,000 Jews will be protected from the trumpet judgments (Rev 7:1-8; 9:4); that they are "caught up to God and to his throne" as the manchild (Rev 12:5; Isa 66:7-8; Dan 12:1); that they are in heaven singing a song that no man can sing but the 144,000 Jews; and that they are in heaven before God 3½ years before the second advent (Rev 14:1-5). Later,

in the fulfillment of these things John saw the tribulation saints singing their song before God in heaven (Rev 15:1-4; 20:4-6). Lastly, he recorded the rapture to heaven of the two witnesses (Rev 11:7-12). All these had been translated to heaven and were there when John saw them. Not only were these in heaven, but without any controversy all the raptured saints are to be literally in heaven before and at the time of the marriage supper, and this will be before the second advent begins (Rev 19:1-21). See many other proofs of the rapture before the tribulation in Chapters 10-11 below.

3. *The third question* asked by the disciples in Mt 24-25 was what would take place at "the end of the world" when Christ would literally land on the planet earth with the raptured saints and angels to set up the kingdom (Mt 24:29-25:46). At the second advent this third question will be fully answered for all. The present partial regathering of Israel precedes the happenings of the above list of signs of the second advent of Christ to the earth. It really is the first sign and the greatest of all signs at the end of this age. The above events could not happen until Israel became a nation, though she will not be fully gathered until after the second advent. See fallacy 5, Chapter 9.

The end of the *world* means the end of this *age,* not the end of mankind or the earth. The Gr. word for world here (Mt 24:3) is *aion,* a period of time whether long or short. It refers here to the age in which we now live, and the one in which Israel rejected the gospel and their Messiah. This age will end at the second advent after the future tribulation. At that time the kingdom will literally come (Acts 1:6-7; Rev 11:15; 19:11-21; 20:4-6). The church age will end at the rapture of the church, and this is before the tribulation, at least 7 years before the second advent. All the events of Rev 4:1-19:10 will precede the second advent of Rev 19:11-21.

28 Major events the first day of the Second Advent:

The following events will begin at the second advent of Christ. The "end of the world" spoken of in Mt 24:3 is the same as mentioned in Mt 13:37-42, 49-50 and it literally means the end of this age in which we now live. The 28 major events are:

1. The one day battle of Armageddon (Zech 14:1-15; Mt 24:29-31; 2 Th 1:7-10; Jude 14-15; Rev 16:13-16; 19:11-21; Joel 2:1-3:25; Isa 64:1-5; 65:1-4; Ezek 38-39)

2. Beasts and birds gathered to eat the carcasses of men slain in the battle (Mt 24:27-28; Lk 17:34-37; Rev 19:17-21; Ezek 39:4, 17-21. Cp Job 39:27-30)

3. Darkness of the sun, moon, and stars (Mt 24:29)

4. Great showers of meteors to the earth (Mt 24:29; Lk 21:25-33; Rev 16:17-21)

5. The powers of the heavens shaken (Mt 24:29; Lk 21:25-33)

6. Sudden appearance of Jesus Christ coming to the earth (Mt 24:30; Rev 1:7)

7. Mourning of all the tribes of the earth (Mt 24:30)

8. Christ coming in power and great glory (Mt 16:27; 24:30; 25:31; 2 Th 1:7-10)

9. Destruction of the armies of earth (Mt 24:32-42; 2 Th 1:7-10; Jude 14-15; Rev 19:11-21; Ezek 38-39; Zech 14; Joel 2-3)

10. The Star and Sceptre shall rise out of Israel – not out of the church – and shall smite many countries (Num 24:17-18; Dt 30:1-10; Ezek 38-39; Zech 14; Rev 19:11-21)

11. The adversaries of the Lord will be completely broken and humbled (1 Sam 2:10; Isa 1:24; 11:13; 59:18; Nah 1:2)

12. Christ will literally and bodily land on the mount of Olives (Zech 14:1-5; Ezek 38-39; Isa 63:1-5; 64:1-5; Joel 2-3; 2 Th 1:7-10; Jude 14-15; Rev 19:11-21)

13. Great changes will be made in the surface of the earth (Isa 35; Ezek 38:20; Zech 14:5, 10; Rev 16:17-21; 18:1-24)

14. Armies of Antichrist will destroy one another (Zech 14:13)

15. The destruction of Antichrist's armies will also be by supernatural power (Zech 14:12; Ezek 38:17-23; Mal 4:1; 2 Th 1:7-10; Rev 19:11-21)

16. Angels will visibly mete out vengenance on the ungodly (2 Th 1:7-10; Mt 13:39-42; 16:27; 24:29-31; 25:31-46)

17. The Antichrist and false prophet will be killed and changed from mortality to immortality and be cast into the lake of fire to remain eternally (Dan 7:11; 2 Th 2:7-8; Rev 19:20; 20:10)

18. Satan, his angels, and demons will be cast into the bottomless pit for 1,000 years (Rev 20:3, 7-10; Isa 24:21-23)

19. Sudden destruction will come upon the ungodly (1 Th 5:1-11; 2 Th 1:7-10; Jude 14-15)

20. All Israel will be born again in one day (Rom 11:25-29; Zech 12:10-13:1; Isa 44:21-23; 45:8, 17; 46:13; 51:6; 59:20-21; 62:11; 66:7-8)

21. Vengeance meted out to all enemies of God on earth (Isa 34:8; 61:2; 63:1-6)

22. Literal Babylon will be destroyed in one hour (Isa 13:19-22; 47:1-17; Jer 5-51; Rev 15:8; 16:17-21; 18:1-24)

23. The Lord will rain fire and brimstone upon all His enemies (Ps 11:6; 97:1-9; Ezek 38:17-21; Rev 16:17-21; Mal 4:1; Mt 24:31; 2 Th 1:7-10)

24. God will give to Israel the 6 things promised them in Daniel's 70th week (Dan 9:24-27). See Chapter 2.

25. This age will come to an end (Mt 12:31-32; 24:14; 29-31; 25:31-46; Lk 20:35; Eph 1:10; 2:7, 3:11; Rev 19:11-21; 20:1-10)

26. The times of the Gentiles will end (Dan 9:27; 12:1-7; Mt 24:31; Lk 21:24; Rev 11:1-2)

27. The great tribulation will end (Dan 9:27; 12:1-7; Mt 24:15-22, 29-31; Rev 11:1-2)

28. The 70th week of Daniel will come to an end (Dan 9:24-27; Mt 24:15-22, 29-31; Rev 19:11-21; Lk 21:24)

Events of the first 75 days after the Second Advent (Dan 12:7-13)
3 Time Periods of Daniel 12:7-13:

(1) The "time, times, and an half" of vs 7, this being the 1,260 days of the last half of Daniel's 70th week (Dan 7:25, 9:27; Rev 11:1-3; 12:6, 14; 13:5)

(2) The "thousand two hundred and ninety days" of vs 11, these 1,290 days evidently allowing an additional 30 days for a clean-up period to rid Jerusalem and the temple site of the abomination of desolation as part of the preparations for the rebuilding of the temple by Christ, Himself (Zech 6:12-13)

(3) The "thousand three hundred five and thirty days" of vs 12, these 1,335 days allowing 45 days still beyond the 1,290, making a total of 75 days from the "abomination of desolation" to the actual proclamation of the kingdom of God and of Christ on earth. In the 75 days, the preparatory events to precede the actual proclamation will include the complete regathering of Israel by the angels (Mt 24:29-31), and the gathering of the nations to the judgment of nations (Mt 25:31-46; Dan 7:9-14). Blessed are the people who will live through the battle of Armageddon and meet the conditions of escaping death at the judgment of the nations and be allowed to enter the kingdom (Mt 25:31-36).

5 Fallacies related to Mt 24-25:

There are some false interpretations of Mt 24-25 and related fallacies that we must warn the reader about in order to make clear the truths of this wonderful prophecy of Jesus Christ.

FALLACY 1: Prophetical Date-setting is Scriptural.

TRUTH: No less than 5 times Christ warned men not to go beyond their knowledge regarding the day and the hour of His coming to the earth (Mt 24:36, 42, 44, 50; 25:13). He said that He did not know the exact time, Himself, and that the Father only knew (Mk 13:32). He told His followers later that the time of the second advent was in the hands of the Father (Acts 1:7). In view of these facts it is foolish to seek to know or to claim to know the exact date of Christ's second coming. Only this much we know: it cannot take place any day *until after* the tribulation (Mt 24:29-31); *until after* the reign of the Antichrist (2 Th 2:7-8; Rev 19:11-21); and *until after* the fulfillment of Rev 4:1-19:10.

FALLACY 2: Two in the field, one taken and the other left refers to the Rapture of the church.

TRUTH: In Mt 24:37-42 we have one of the most misunderstood scriptures, and the errors of interpretation related thereto are being perpetuated by the daily preaching of many who have never come to know the truth. Take, for instance, the statement of "two in the field, one shall be taken and another left," which is so commonly taught as referring to the rapture. Instead, those "taken" is a reference to those who will be killed or destroyed or taken away in the battle of Armageddon, the comparison being "the flood came, and TOOK THEM ALL AWAY" or destroyed them, "so shall also the coming of the Son of man be." Multitudes of men will be killed in this battle and will make up the "carcasses" or the dead bodies for the beasts and birds to eat, as described in Mt 24:28; Lk 17:34-37; Rev 19:17-21; Ezek 39:4, 17-21.

FALLACY 3: The fig tree represents the Jewish nation (Mt 24:32).

TRUTH: Seldom, if ever, is this scripture properly used and understood as Jesus intended it to be. It is nearly always used as representing the Jewish nation instead of being recognized as a literal fig tree used to illustrate the nearness of Christ's return, as plainly stated. Men generally refer to the budding fig tree as the Jewish nation and use ten to fifteen leaves of the tree to promote the teaching of the rebuilding of Israel as a nation. But this is far from the true idea. Here, in Mt 24:32 Jesus used only the fig tree in His illustration, but in Lk 21:29 He said, "Behold the fig tree, and ALL THE TREES," when illustrating the nearness of His return. He said that "When THEY (the fig tree and all the other trees) now shoot forth" with their leaves in the springtime everyone knows that summer is near, SO LIKEWISE, when we see the signs of the second advent (listed above; see page 45) beginning to come to pass, THEN we should recognize the nearness of His return to the earth to set up His kingdom (Lk 21:31).

FALLACY 4: The parable of the ten virgins proves that one must have the oil of the Spirit baptism in order to go in the rapture which will take place at midnight.

TRUTH: Every detail of the parable of the ten virgins is part of a story or an illustration used to show the importance of *watchfulness* in view of the second advent of Christ to the earth with His saints to fight, conquer, and rule (Mt 25:13). As in any other illustration, the details are needed to make up the story of the happening or event which is used to illustrate something, but after the intended truth is conveyed the details have no further meaning, for they have fulfilled their purpose. The parables of Mt 24 and 25 are illustrations used in connection with the second advent to teach: nearness, readiness, faithfulness, watchfulness, and diligence.

FALLACY 5: The judgment of Mt 25:31-46 is the same as the judgment seat of Christ of 2 Cor 5:10.

TRUTH: This scripture — Mt 25:31-46 — does not refer to the judgment seat of Christ at all, but rather to the judgment of the living nations that are on earth when Christ lands here at the end of this age. This judgment will determine who among men are worthy of entering the earthly kingdom of Christ at that time, thus completing an answer to the question of what will take place at the second advent which will bring this age to an end, and begin the Millennium (Dan 7:9-14; 12:12; Mt 25:31-46). Not one word is said here of the church, its rapture, its judgment, or work on earth. The ones at this judgment are simply permitted to enter the kingdom, or sent to hell. Those who enter the kingdom will continue as earthly subjects of Christ who will begin His rule of the earth at this time.

Two Important Questions Answered:

1. *How do we know that Israel and not the church* is being dealt with in Mt 24-25? We know from the following facts and scriptures:

(1) Jesus is speaking to Jews and answering Jewish questions concerning earthly and political events regarding Israel. The questions concern the Jewish Messiah and His coming back to earth to deliver the Jews from the Gentiles and to set up their long predicted Jewish kingdom on earth (Mt 24:3; 25:34, 46; Lk 1:32-33; 12:32; 22:29; Acts 1:6; Joel 2-3; Zech 14; Rev 11:15).

(2) The deceptions by false Christs and messiahs of Mt 24:5, 23-26 concern Israel, not the church. Jesus definitely predicted that Israel would be so deceived (Jn 5:43).

(3) The sign of anti-semitism of Mt 24:9 refers to Israel only.

(4) The term "sorrows" (literally the travail of Israel) of Mt 24:8, 15-22; Isa 66:7-8; Jer 30:7; Dan 12:1; Rev 12:6, 14) refers to Israel only.

(5) The defeat of the nation of Israel and her flight into the wilderness of Mt 24:15-22; Isa 16:1-5; Ezek 20:33-44; Hos 2:14-18; Dan 11:40-43; Rev 12:2, 14 are a reference to Israel only.

(6) The flight of Israel *from Judea* is definitely Jewish (Mt 24:15-16).

(7) The abomination of desolation set up in the Jewish temple at Jerusalem will be solely Jewish in fulfillment (Mt 24:15; Dan 9:24; 2 Th 2:1-4).

(8) Keeping the sabbath day and a reference to fleeing from Antichrist on this day can only be understood in connection with Israel, not the church. Church people would never feel restricted in their travels on that day; even travelling hundreds and thousands of miles on the sabbath day would be acceptable with them (Mt 24:20).

(9) The great tribulation of Mt 24:21-22 is particularly Jewish in fulfillment even though many Gentiles will also suffer (Isa 66:7-8; Jer 30:7; Dan 9:27; 12:1; Rev 12:6, 14-17).

(10) The "elect" of Mt 24:22, 31 is the Jewish elect because they live in "Judea." This could not refer to the church, for the church is not concentrated in the land of Judea.

(11) The predicted battle of Armageddon of Mt 24:28, 37-43; Lk 17:34-38; Rev 19:17-21; Ezek 39:4, 17-21; Zech 14 concerns only Israel and their city of Jerusalem – not the church with its numerous and various headquarters locations. Nothing is said of the Christian church fighting at Jerusalem as is said of the Jews (Zech 14:14).

(12) The gospel (good news) of the kingdom in Mt 24:14 is primarily Jewish and it refers to the good news that the kingdom of David and of Israel will soon be established in Jerusalem (Isa 9:6-7; 59:20-21; Jer 30; Ezek 34:23-31; 27:24-28; Lk 1:32-33; Acts 15:13-18; Rev 11:15; 20:4-6; Dan 2:44-45; 7:9-14, 18, 22, 27; Zech 14).

(13) The 70th week of Dan 9:27 concerns only "thy people (Israel) and thy holy city (Jerusalem)" and will be fulfilled with Jews only (Mt 24:4-31; Lk 21:6-11, 25-33; 2 Th 2; Rev 4:1-19:21). The church is not once mentioned in any of these scriptures.

(14) The temple of God wherein Antichrist places the abomination of desolation as in Mt 24:15 is wholly Jewish and in fulfillment will have nothing to do with the church or any church building (Dan 9:27; 2 Th 2:1-4; Rev 11:1-2).

(15) The coming of Christ at His second advent referred to in Mt 24:29-31 primarily concerns earthly Israel (the church saints having already been raptured by then), and Israel's deliverance from Antichrist and his followers at the battle of Armageddon, at which time the salvation of Israel and the possession of the earth by Christ and Israel will be accomplished (Dan 9:27; 12:1; Zech 14; 2 Th 1:7-10; Jude 14-15; Rev 19:11-21).

2. *Are all the signs of the second advent given in Mt 24-25 to be fulfilled in one particular generation,* or will the fulfillment be scattered events throughout the entire age? That the fulfillment will be in one particular generation only, at the end of this age is clear:

(1) In Mt 24:33-34 we are told that "when ye shall see all these things, know that it (the second advent of Christ) is near . . . . This generation shall not pass, till all these things be fulfilled." The term "this generation" is used 16 times in the N. T. and every time of a particular span of life and not of a race of people as some teach (Mt 11:16; 12:41-42; 23:36; 24:34; Mk 8:12; 13:30; Lk 7:31; 11:30, 31, 32, 50, 51; 17:25; 21:32). The reference then cannot be to various events happening throughout the history of Israel, for this race as

well as all other races of people are eternal and will continue in the
new earth (Rev 21-22; Dan 7:9-14; Zech 14). They will not pass
away, so the "generation" that "shall not pass, till all these things be
fulfilled," can only refer to a span of life.

(2) "The days of Noah" refers to only one generation — a span of
life used in comparison with the days wherein the signs of the second
advent would be taking place (Mt 24:37-39; Gen 7:1).

(3) In speaking of the end-time Jesus referred to a particular
generation when He predicted that some "shall endure unto the end"
and "be saved" (Mt 24:13). And again, in Lk 21:34-36 when He
urged watchfulness and prayer to "be accounted worthy to escape all
these things that shall come to pass," the reference had to be to a
particular generation of people whose life span would be taking place
at the time "these things" would be coming to pass.

Chapter 7

Rapture of the Church and O. T. saints

1. *The Fact and Manner of the Rapture*

There are about 50 scriptures in the N. T. and some related ones in the O. T. that reveal the fact and manner of the rapture, or the transporting to heaven of all the "dead and living in Christ" at this point. They also reveal WHEN this event will take place, that is, when in connection with various end-time events. The following quotations are not all the scriptures pertaining to a definite rapture separate and distinct from the second advent, but they are enough to prove the doctrine of a rapture beyond doubt:

(1) "Watch ye therefore, and pray always, that ye may be accounted worthy TO ESCAPE ALL THESE THINGS that shall come to pass, and TO STAND BEFORE THE SON OF MAN" (Lk 21:34-36). "All these things" that worthy saints will escape are the events of ALL THE SIGNS of the second advent listed in Lk 21:4-11, 25-33; Mt 24:4-28; Mk 13:4-27; 2 Th 2:1-12; Rev 4:1-19:21. (See Chapter 10.) This means that ALL THESE THINGS which saints escape by being raptured to stand before the Son of man will all take place after they are raptured to the place where the Son of man is. There will be *first* the meeting with Him in the air (1 Th 4:13-18), and *secondly* a journey to heaven and a meeting with the Father in heaven itself (Col 4:4; 1 Th 3:13, 5:23; Jas 5:7-8; Rev 5:8-10; 19:1-10).

(2) "In my Father's house (the Holy City in heaven where He lives) are many mansions: if it were not so, I would have told you. I go to prepare a place for you. And if I go and prepare a place for you, I will come again, and receive you unto myself; that where I am, there ye may be also" (Jn 14:1-3). If we are going to be RECEIVED by Christ to Himself; if we are going to be received into the Father's house to live in mansions so that where He lives we may live also; and if all of this takes place at the time Christ comes from heaven to take us up to heaven, then there is truly going to be a rapture before the second advent. It is absolutely necessary in order for us to eat a supper, the marriage supper of the Lamb in heaven (Jn 14:1-3; Rev 19:1-21) before the second advent begins — before we are predicted to come back WITH Him at the time of His second advent.

(3) "But every man in his own order (company or rank): Christ the firstfruits; afterward (at the next general rapture) they that are Christ's at his coming" (1 Cor 15:23). This shows us that there are

different orders or ranks and companies of resurrected people, and means that every man who belongs to Christ will go in his own company.

(4) "Behold, I show you a mystery: We shall not all sleep (die), but we shall be changed . . . . In a moment, in the twinkling of an eye, at the last trump: for the trumpet shall sound, and the dead (in Christ, 1 Th 4:16) shall be raised incorruptible, and we (the living in Christ, also 1 Th 4:16) shall be changed . . . . For this corruptible must put on incorruption, and this mortal must put on immortality . . . so when this corruptible shall have put on incorruption, and this mortal shall have put on immortality, then shall be brought to pass the saying that is written, Death is swallowed up in victory. O death, where is thy sting? O grave, where is thy victory?" (1 Cor 15:51-56). When this scripture is fulfilled the saints will be raptured to meet the Lord in the air (1 Th 4:13-18), and then they will be taken on to heaven to be presented before God (1 Th 2:19-20; 3:13; 5:23; Jas 5:7-8; Col 3:4). For a study on the "last" trump not being the same as the 7th trumpet that will sound in the tribulation period, see fallacy 10, Chapter 9.

(5) "That he might present it to himself a glorious church, not having spot, or wrinkle, or any such thing; but that it should be holy and without blemish" (Eph 5:27). This refers to the personal visible meeting of Christ and His saints in the air, at the time when He comes to take them to heaven to their mansions, as stated above in point (2).

(6) "But I would not have you to be ignorant, brethren, concerning them which are asleep, that ye sorrow not, even as others which have no hope. For if we believe that Jesus died and rose again, even so them also which sleep (have died) in Jesus will God bring with him. For this we say unto you by the word of the Lord, that we which are alive and remain unto the coming of the Lord shall not prevent (precede) them which are asleep (dead). For the Lord himself shall descend from heaven with a shout, with the voice of the archangel, and with the trump of God (not the trump of one of the 7 trumpet angels of Revelation): and the dead in Christ shall rise first: then we which are alive and remain SHALL BE CAUGHT UP together with them in the clouds TO MEET THE LORD IN THE AIR; and so shall we ever be with the Lord" (1 Th 4:13-18).

(7) "The mystery of iniquity doth already work: only he who now letteth (hindereth) will let (hinder lawlessness and hold back the coming of Antichrist), UNTIL he (the hinderer of lawlessness) be TAKEN OUT OF THE WAY. AND THEN (and not before) shall that Wicked (the lawless one, the Antichrist) be revealed, whom the Lord shall consume with the spirit of his mouth, and shall destroy with the brightness of his coming" (2 Th 2:7-8). This says plainly that the one

who hinders lawlessness and the revelation of the Antichrist will continue to hinder UNTIL he is taken out of the way to hinder no more; AND THEN, and only THEN, will the man of sin be revealed. This refers to the rapture of the church before the revelation of Antichrist, and there can be no doubt of this, as proved fully in Chapter 10, Proof 1, below.

(8) "WHEN Christ, who is our life, shall appear, THEN shall ye also appear with him in glory" (Col 3:4). This "glory" refers to heaven, itself, and not to the earth; and so, if we go to heaven at that point we are ascending to glory rather than descending from heaven with Christ to the earth as we are predicted to be doing at the second advent. Glory indicates the presence of God (Ezek 10:4, 18-19; 11:22-23; 43:2-5; 44:4). Glory is a heavenly place (1 Pet 5:10; 2 Pet 1:17; Jude 24). Glory is also a substance (Rev 15:8; 18:1; 21:23; Lk 2:9; 9:32; Jn 12:41; Acts 7:55; 22:11; 1 Cor 2:8; Col 3:4). God is called the King of glory (Ps 24:8-10). Saints are to go to glory (Ps 73:24; Col 3:4). Both God and Christ will appear in glory (Ps 102:16; Col 3:4). Raptured saints are to go to heaven and be there for several years before leaving that glory for the earth with Christ at His second advent (Rev 19:1-21).

(9) "God hath not appointed us to wrath (the tribulation wrath of God of 1 Th 5:1-11; Rev 6:17-16:21; 19:15), but to obtain salvation (deliverance from that wrath by rapture) by our Lord Jesus Christ; who died for us, that whether we wake (live in the body) or sleep (die), we should live (be resurrected in body) together with him" (1 Th 5:9-11). If God will thus deliver us from the coming wrath, He will do so by the rapture, taking us to heaven and fulfilling all the scriptures.

(10) "Behold, the husbandman (the Father, Jn 15:1-8) waiteth for the precious fruit of the earth, and hath long patience for it, until he receive the early and latter rain" (Jas 5:7-8). When will He do this? When Christ comes "to receive us unto" Himself, as He promised in Jn 14:1-3. Saints will thus be taken to heaven to be presented to the Father before coming back to the earth with Christ (1 Th 3:13; 5:23).

As stated before, there are about 50 scriptures — around 40 besides the above — that teach the rapture of all saints to heaven in the first resurrection (1 Cor 1:8; 2 Cor 5:1-10; Phil 3:10-11, 21; 1 Th 1:10; 2:19-20; 3:13; 5:23; 2 Th 2:1-12; 1 Tim 6:14; 2 Tim 4:1, 8; Tit 2:13; Heb 11:10-16; 12:22-23; 13:14; 1 Pet 1:5, 7, 9, 11, 13; 4:13; 5:1-8; 2 Pet 1:3; Jude 24; 1 Jn 2:28; 3:2; Rev 5:8-10; 11:7-12; 12:5; 14:1-5; 15:1-4; 19:1-10; 20:4-8 Dan 12:1; Isa 66:7-8; Ps 73:24; 23:6; 102:16; Rom 8:18).

Let it be remembered that in the fulfillment of the THINGS WHICH MUST BE AFTER THE CHURCHES of Rev 4:1-22:5, there are several companies of raptured saints seen in heaven by John, such as those in Rev 5:8-10; 6:9-11; 7:9-17; 12:5; 14:1-5; 15:1-4; 20:4-6 and the two witnesses of Rev 11:7-12. In Rev 19:1-10 all these companies of raptured saints are seen in heaven eating a marriage supper with Christ just before the second advent begins (Rev 19:11-21). They are the ones who will come with Christ all the way between heaven and earth (Zech 14:5; Rev 19:14).

2. *The Rapture an "out-resurrection" from the Dead*

In Phil 3:11 the rapture is called "the resurrection of the dead," or literally, "the out resurrection," meaning the resurrection of some of the dead from among the dead. A general resurrection of all the dead at one time without a time between the resurrection of the just and the resurrection of the unjust seems to be taught in Dan 12:2; Jn 5:28-29; Acts 24:18; but in the final revelation on the subject we learn that there will actually be 1,000 years between the first resurrection of the just, and the second resurrection of the unjust (Rev 20:11-15). We can now, at the present time, have a choice regarding which resurrection to be in — whether we want to be saved and in the first, or lost and in the second (Mk 26:15-16; Jn 3:16). This is what Paul had in mind when he wanted to be in the "out-resurrection" from among the wicked dead (Phil 3:11).

3. *There are 40 purposes of the Rapture*

1. For Christ to receive the saints of all past ages to Himself (Jn 14:1-3)

2. To take all raptured saints to heaven (Jn 14:1-3; 1 Th 3:13; 4:13-18)

3. To meet the saints in the air (1 Th 4:13-18)

4. To settle the saints in their mansions (Jn 14:1-3; Heb 11:10-16; 12:22-23; 13:14)

5. To bring great joy to soul winners (1 Th 2:19-20; 2 Cor 1:14)

6. To present the saints to God in heaven (1 Th 3:13)

7. To make the saints whole in body, soul, and spirit (1 Th 5:23)

8. To judge the saints at the judgment seat of Christ (Rom 14:10-12; 1 Cor 3:11-15; 2 Cor 5:10; Phil 3:10-11; 2 Tim 4:1, 8)

9. To confirm saints blameless (1 Cor 1:8; 1 Th 3:13; 5:23)

10. To assign positions as kings and priests to rule all creations (1 Cor 6:1-3; Lk 22:30; Rev 1:5; 2:26-27; 5:10; Dan 7:1-27)

11. To resurrect all saints of the N.T. and O.T. times (1 Cor 15:23, 35-44; 2 Cor 4:14; Phil 3:11; Dan 12:2; Jn 5:28-29; 1 Th 4:13-18; Rev 20:4-6)

12. To change saints from mortality to immortality (1 Cor 15:51-56; Phil 3:21)

13. To reward saints with different glories (1 Cor 15:23, 35-44)

14. To give saints victory over death, hell, and the grave (1 Cor 15:51-56)

15. To give saints everlasting life (Gal 6:7-9)

16. To show saints God's eternal riches and grace (Eph 2:7, 3:11)

17. To give saints their inherited kingdom (1 Cor 6:9-11; Eph 5:5-6; Gal 5:19-21)

18. To present the church to Himself (Eph 5:27)

19. To complete the work started in saints (Phil 1:6)

20. To change the vile bodies of saints (Phil 3:21)

21. To appear with saints in glory (Col 3:4)

22. To permit the coming of the man of sin (2 Th 2:7-8)

23. To give saints a crown of righteousness (2 Tim 4:8)

24. To give saints the reality of the blessed hope (Tit 2:13)

25. To take saints to the New Jerusalem to live (Heb 11:10-16; 12:22-23; 13:14; Jn 14:1-3)

26. To receive the fruit of the early and latter rain (Jas 5:7-8)

27. To give saints final salvation and grace (1 Pet 1:5, 7, 9, 13)

28. To give saints a reckoning day (1 Pet 4:5-6)

29. To reveal the glory of God and Christ to saints (1 Pet 4:13)

30. To give saints an abundant entrance into the kingdom (2 Pet 1:11)

31. To make saints confident and unashamed (1 Jn 2:28)

32. To make saints like Christ (1 Jn 3:2)

33. To reveal Christ to saints as He actually is (1 Jn 3:2)

34. To fulfill with saints all the promises to believers (Rev 2:7, 11, 17, 26-27; 3:5, 11-12, 21; 2 Pet 1:4; 2 Cor 1:20)

35. To take saints out of the earth for the duration of the tribulation (Lk 21:34-36)

36. To end the church age and make it possible for God to deal more exclusively with Israel to fulfill with them the latter day prophecies (Dan 9:27; 11:4-45; Zech 12:1-14:15; Mt 24-25; Lk 21:1-11, 25-33; 2 Th 2; Rev 1:19; 4:1. See Chapter 10.)

37. To free saints from the coming wrath of God (1 Th 5:1-11)

38. To take the hinderer of lawlessness out of the world (2 Th 2:7-8)

39. To give church saints at least 7 years to live in heaven, to become acquainted with the future life, and prepare for earth rulership (Jn 14:1-3; Dan 9:27; Eph 2:7; 3:11)

40. To have the saints in heaven to partake of the marriage supper and to accompany Christ back to earth to fight at Armageddon (Rev 19:1-21; Zech 14:1-5; Mt 24:29-31; 2 Th 1:7-10; 2:7-8; Jude 14-15). If there would be no rapture until the second advent, then all of these above mentioned purposes would be cancelled.

4. *The 10 qualifications for the Rapture:*

(1) *One must be in Christ:* "the dead *in Christ* shall rise first: then we which are alive (in Christ) and remain shall be caught up together to meet the Lord in the air; and so shall we ever be with the Lord" (1 Th 4:13-18). To "be in Christ" means that we are a new creature; old things are passed away; all things are become new; and all things are of God, who hath reconciled us into Himself (2 Cor 5:17-21).

(2) *One must belong to Christ:* "But every man in his own order: Christ the firstfruits; afterward *they that are Christ's* at his coming" (1 Cor 15:23). To belong to Christ means that we "have crucified the flesh with the affections and lusts" (Gal 5:24).

(3) *One must do good:* "all that are in the graves ahall hear his voice, and shall come forth; they that have done good, unto the resurrection of life; and they that have done evil, unto the resurrection of damnation" (Jn 5:28-29).

(4) *One must be blessed and holy:* "Blessed and holy is he that hath part in the first resurrection; on such the second death hath no power, but they shall be priests of God and of Christ" (Rev 20:4-6; Heb 12:14).

(5) *One must be worthy:* "Watch ye therefore, and pray always, that ye may be accounted worthy to escape ALL THESE THINGS (of Lk 21:6-11, 25-33; Mt 24-25; Rev 4:1-18:24; 2 Th 2; 1 Th 5; etc.) that shall come to pass (in the tribulation), and TO STAND BEFORE THE SON OF MAN" (Lk 21:34-36).

(6) *One must be in the church:* "For by one Spirit are we all baptized into one body, whether we be Jews or Gentiles" (1 Cor 12:13, 27; Eph 1:22-23; Col 1:18, 24).

(7) *One must be pure:* "Beloved, now are we the sons of God, and it doth not yet appear what we shall be: but we know that, when he shall appear, we shall be like him; for we shall see him as he is. And every man that hath this hope in him purifieth himself, EVEN AS HE IS PURE" (1 Jn 3:2-3).

(8) *One must be without spot or wrinkle... and without blemish:* "That he might present it to himself a glorious church, not having spot, or wrinkle, or any such thing; but that it should be holy and without blemish" (Eph 5:27).

(9) *One must live and walk in the Spirit:* "ye shall not fulfill the lust of the flesh," (Gal 5:16).... "Now the works of the flesh are manifest, which are these: adultery, fornication, uncleanness, lasciviousness, idolatry, witchcraft, hatred, variance, emulations, wrath, strife, seditions, heresies, envyings, murders, drunkenness, revellings, and such like... they which do such things shall not inherit the kingdom of God" — and will not go up in the rapture (Gal 5:19-21).

(10) *One must walk in the light:* "But if we walk in the light, as he is in the light, we have fellowship one with another, and the blood of Jesus Christ cleanseth us from all sin" (1 Jn 1:7; Col 2:6-7).

5. *The Rapture is not a part of the Second Advent*

The common theory that the second coming of Christ is in two parts and that it will take place in two stages, or in two phases, and that there is only one coming of Christ out of heaven, is completely false and unscriptural. There are two definite comings of Jesus Christ out of heaven and not two parts of one coming. The rapture is the coming of Christ from heaven to the clouds surrounding the earth, but He does not come to the earth at that time. He simply resurrects the righteous dead and catches them up to Himself in the clouds and then takes them on into heaven with Him to remain there during the tribulation period after which He and the resurrected righteous ones will return to the earth and land on the earth as a second advent event. At His first coming He literally landed on earth to live here and die for men. At His second coming He will also literally land on the earth again, and live here to reign (Zech 14:4). The rapture, then, could never be the second coming, and it should never be called the second coming of Christ. No person is ever to be raptured at the second coming to the earth.

The rapture is a complete round trip for Jesus − from heaven to the clouds around the earth, and back again to heaven. It is the time when He comes FOR the saints in the air, and when they are caught up to the clouds with Him. He then returns with them to heaven to live there at least 7 years before the second advent begins. All raptures will be completed before the second advent begins. They will take all the saints to heaven whereas the second advent will bring them all back from heaven to the earth to set up a kingdom to be ruled by Christ, His angels, and the raptured saints.

6. *The time of the Rapture*

The time of the rapture, like that of the second advent, is not definitely known as to the day or the hour, but we do know that it will take place *before* the tribulation, *before* the reign of Antichrist, *before* the fulfillment of Mt 24-25; Rev 4:1-22:5, and *before* the fulfillment of many other prophecies, as proved in Chapters 10-11 below, which see.

There are a number of scriptures in the Bible that make it crystal clear that the rapture will take place before the tribulation. Here are a few examples from Christ and the N. T. writers:

1. Jesus Christ plainly urged us to "Watch . . . and pray always, that ye may be accounted worthy TO ESCAPE ALL THESE THINGS (of the tribulation of Lk 21:1-11, 25-33) that shall come to

pass, and to stand before the Son of Man" (Lk 21:34-36).

It would be a false promise of Christ, to His disciples of this whole church age, if no "worthy" saints are to escape the last day events of the tribulation. It would be truly needless and give a false hope for anyone to pray to escape "ALL these things" if nobody is to escape them. The promise is clear here that all worthy ones WILL ESCAPE going through *all these things* and will literally be "caught up" to meet the Lord in the air and "TO STAND BEFORE THE SON OF MAN." Saints could not possibly stand before the Son of man until the time when He comes to "receive you unto myself" (Jn 14:1-3), and to "meet the Lord in the air," which will be at the time of the rapture (1 Th 4:13-16).

2. Paul said that the church—the hinderer of lawlessness—will be removed before the revelation of the Antichrist (2 Th 2:5-10). See Chapter 10, proof 1.

3. John was definitely told by Christ to "come up hither" and "I will show thee things which must be hereafter," that is, after the churches (Rev 1:19; 4:1). See Chapter 10, proof 2.

Besides the above, the four exclusive raptures (see Chapter 11) also confirm the fact of the rapture of the church before the tribulation and Daniel's 70th week.

Chapter 8

The Second Coming of Jesus Christ

Before taking up the fallacies about the rapture and the time of the rapture, we must understand the doctrine of the second advent itself. The second advent is the time when Christ will come to the earth *with* the saints, and this is the coming that will take place immediately *after* the tribulation (Mt 24:29-31; 25:31-46; Rev 19:11-21; Zech 14; Jude 14-15). We must understand that the rapture is not one stage, one phase, or one part of the second coming of Christ to the earth, but that it is a separate and distinct coming from heaven *for* the saints *before* the future tribulation and *before* the last 7 years of this age, and *before* Antichrist comes. It is at least 7 years *before* the second coming of Christ which will end this age and usher in the Millennium.

1. *Second Advent not part of the Rapture*

The second coming of Christ is one of the greatest events of the entire Bible. It is one of the chief themes of Scripture, as we shall see. A brief study, which follows, will enable the reader to get a clear understanding of the subject.

As a young Bible student 18 years of age I used to become confused by the average minister's preaching on the second advent and the rapture. Almost without exception these persons would refer to the rapture and the second advent as the same event, using both terms interchangeably of the one coming of Christ, there being as they supposed, two parts, two stages, and two phases of the one coming. They would point to the many signs of the second advent, or rapture, and tell how the tribulation and 7-year reign of Antichrist would have to take place before the second advent or rapture, then make a plea for persons not ready for the event to meet at the altar of prayer immediately. The reason given for such urgency was that the rapture could take place that night — perhaps even before the people could get down to the altar.

I could never reconcile the conflicting statements — that there should be 7 years of tribulation and the reign of Antichrist before the coming of Christ, and yet it could happen "tonight." What these teachers should have said was that the rapture and the second advent were two distinct subjects, the events being unrelated to each other, and that whereas the rapture could take place "tonight" the second advent could not take place until after the tribulation and the last 7 years of this age which would include the reign of Antichrist. It is still truth to teach that the rapture could take place now at any moment. As to the second advent it must be understood that this event cannot take place until after the tribulation and the reign of Antichrist. In fact, all the prophecies of Mt 24-25; Mk 13; Lk 21:1-11, 25-33; 2 Th 2; 1 Th 5; Rev 4:1-19:10 must be fulfilled in detail *before* the second advent of Christ and *after* the rapture.

2. *The Fact and Manner of the Second Advent*

The second coming of Christ is vividly described in many scriptures from Genesis to Revelation as follows:

Testimony of 21 O. T. prophets

1. *Enoch:* "Behold, the Lord cometh with ten thousands of his saints, to execute judgment upon all, and to convince all that are ungodly among them of all their ungodly deeds which they have ungodly committed, and of all their hard speeches which the ungodly sinners have spoken against him" (Jude 14-15).

2. *Jacob:* "The sceptre shall not depart from Judah, nor a lawgiver from between his feet until Shiloh come; and unto him shall the gathering of the people be" (Gen 49:10).

3. *Balaam:* "There shall come a Star out of Jacob, and a Sceptre shall rise out of Israel, and shall smite the corners of Moab . . . out of Jacob shall come he that shall have dominion" (Num 24:17-19).

4. *Moses:* "The Lord shall return and gather thee from all nations, whither the Lord thy God hath scattered thee" (Dt. 30:1-11).

5. *Job:* "I know that my Redeemer liveth, and that he shall stand at the latter day upon the earth" (Job 19:25-27).

6. *David:* "The kingdom is the Lord's; and he is Governor among the nations . . . . In his day shall the righteous flourish; and abundance of peace so long as the moon endureth. He shall have dominion also from sea to sea, and from the river unto the ends of the earth" (Ps 22:26-31; 72:1-17; 110:1-7).

7. *Ethan:* "I will make him, my firstborn, higher than the kings of the earth" (Ps 89:27).

8. *A Psalmist:* "When the Lord shall build up Zion, he shall appear in his glory" (Ps 102:16). See Ezek 36:1-37:28.

9. *Isaiah:* "The Redeemer shall come to Zion, and unto them that turn transgression from Jacob" (Isa 59:20); "of the increase of his government and peace there shall be no end. Upon the throne of David, and upon his kingdom, to order it, and to establish it with judgment and with justice from henceforth even for ever" (Isa 9:6-7); "Behold, the Lord God will come with strong hand, and his arm shall rule for him" (Isa 40:9-11); "Who is this that cometh from

Edom, with dyed garments from Bozrah? this that is glorious in apparel, traveling in the greatness of his strength? I that speak in righteousness, mighty to save. Wherefore art thou red in thine apparel, and thy garments like him that treadeth in the winefat? I have trodden the winepress alone; and of the people there was none with me: for I will tread them in mine anger, and trample them in my fury; and their blood shall be sprinkled upon my garments, and I will stain all my raiment. For the day of vengeance is in mine heart, and the year of my redeemed is come" (Isa 63:1-4; Rev 14:14-20; 19:15); "For, behold, the Lord will come with fire and with his chariots like a whirlwind, to render his anger with fury, and his rebuke with flames of fire. For by fire and by sword will the Lord plead with all flesh: and the slain of the Lord shall be many . . . . For I know their works and their thoughts: it shall come, that I will gather all nations and tongues; and they shall come, and see my glory" (Isa 66:15-21).

10. *Jeremiah:* "At that time they shall call Jerusalem the throne of the Lord; and all nations shall be gathered unto it, to the name of the Lord, to Jerusalem; neither shall they walk any more after the imagination of their evil heart" (Jer 3:14-25); "The days come, saith the Lord, that I will raise unto David a righteous Branch, and a King shall reign and prosper, and shall execute judgment and justice in the earth. In his day Judah shall be saved, and Israel shall dwell safely: and this is his name whereby he shall be called, THE LORD OUR RIGHTEOUSNESS" (Jer 23:5-6). See also Jer 25:30-33; 30:3-24; 31:1-9, 27-40; 32:37-44; 33:3-26; 50:19-20.

11. *Ezekiel:* "I will call for a sword against him . . . every man's sword shall be against his neighbor. And I will plead against him with pestilence and with blood; and I will rain upon him, and upon the many people that are with him, an overflowing rain, and great hailstones, fire and brimstone. Thus will I magnify myself, and sanctify myself; and I will be known in the eyes of many nations, and they shall know that I am the Lord. And I will set my glory among the heathen, and all the heathen shall see my judgment that I have executed, and my hand that I have laid upon them" (Ezek 38:19-23; 39:21). See also Ezek 11:17-21; 20:33-44; 30:1-9; 34:11-31; 36:1-38; 37:1-28.

12. *Daniel:* "I saw . . . one like the Son of man came with the clouds of heaven, and came to the Ancient of days, and they brought him near before him. And there was given him dominion, and glory, and a kingdom, that all people, nations, and languages, should serve him: his dominion is an everlasting dominion, which shall not pass away, and his kingdom that which shall not be destroyed" (Dan 2:44-45; 7:9-14, 18, 22, 27).

13. *Hosea:* "The children of Israel shall abide many days without a king, and without a prince, and without a sacrifice, and without an image, and without an ephod, and without a terraphim. Afterward shall the children of Israel return, and seek the Lord their God, and David their king; and shall fear the Lord and his goodness in the latter days" (Hos. 3:4-5); "I will go and return to my place, till they acknowledge their offence, and seek my face . . . I will not return to destroy Ephraim . . . I will be thy King" (Hos 5:15; 11:9; 13:10).

14. *Joel:* "The day of the Lord cometh . . . . A day of darkness and gloominess, a day of clouds, and of thick darkness . . . . The Lord shall utter his voice before his army . . . the heavens shall shake: but the Lord will be the hope of his people Israel" (Joel 2:1-11; 13:14-17, 20-21).

15. *Amos:* "The Lord shall roar out of Zion. . . . In that day will I raise up the tabernacle of David that is fallen down . . . I will build it up as in the days of old" (Amos 1:2; 9:11-15; Acts 15:13-18).

16. *Obadiah:* "The day of the Lord is upon all nations . . . upon mount Zion shall be deliverance. . . . The house of Jacob shall possess their possessions. . . . Saviours shall come upon mount Zion to judge the mount of Esau; and the kingdom shall be the Lord's" (Obad 15-21).

17. *Micah:* "For, behold, the Lord cometh forth out of his place, and shall come down, and tread upon the high places of the earth. . . . Many nations shall come, and say, Come, and let us go up to the mountain of the Lord, and to the house of the God of Jacob; and he will teach us his ways, and we will walk in his paths: for the law shall go forth of Zion, and the word of the Lord from Jerusalem. He shall judge among many people, and rebuke strong nations afar off; and they shall beat their swords into plowshares, and their spears into pruninghooks: nation shall not lift up a sword against nation, neither shall they learn war any more . . . the Lord shall reign over them in mount Zion from henceforth, even for ever" (Mic 4:1-7; Isa 2:2-4).

18. *Zephaniah:* "Hold thy peace at the presence of the Lord God: for the day of the Lord is at hand. That day is a day of wrath, a day of trouble and distress, a day of wasteness and desolation, a day of darkness and gloominess, a day of clouds and swift darkness. A day of the trumpet and alarm against the fenced cities, and against the high towers . . . that I may assemble the kingdoms, to pour out mine indignation, even all my fierce anger: for all the earth shall be devoured with the fire of my jealousy. The King of Israel, even the Lord, is in the midst of thee: thou shalt not see evil any more" (Zeph 1:7-18; 3:8-20).

19. *Haggai:* "Yet once, it is a little while, and I will shake the heavens, and the earth, and the sea, and the dry land. And I will

shake all nations, and the desire of all nations shall come: and I will fill this house with glory ... I will overthrow the throne of kingdoms, and I will destroy the strength of the kingdoms of the heathen; and I will overthrow the chariots, and those that ride in them; and the horses and their riders shall come down, every one by the sword of his brother" (Hag 2:6-9, 21-23).

20. *Zechariah:* "I come, and I will dwell in the midst of thee, saith the Lord. I am returned to Zion; and will dwell in the midst of Jerusalem: and Jerusalem shall be called a city of truth" (Zech 8:3-8, 20-23); "Behold, I will make Jerusalem a cup of trembling unto all people round about, when they shall be in the siege both against Judah and against Jerusalem ... all people of the earth shall be gathered against it.... In that day shall the Lord defend the inhabitants of Jerusalem.... I will seek to destroy all the nations that come against Jerusalem" (Zech 12:1-13:9); "Behold, the day of the Lord cometh, and thy spoil shall be divided in the midst of thee. For I will gather all nations against Jerusalem to battle; and the city shall be taken ... half of the city shall go forth into captivity, and the residue of the people shall not be cut off from the city. Then shall the Lord go forth, and fight against those nations, as when he fought in the day of battle. And his feet shall stand in that day upon the mount of Olives, which is before Jerusalem on the east, and the mount of Olives shall cleave in the midst thereof toward the east and toward the west ... half of the mountain shall remove toward the north, and half of it toward the south ... the Lord my God shall come, and all the saints with thee. And the Lord shall be king over all the earth. And this shall be the plague wherewith the Lord will smite all the people that have fought against Jerusalem. Their flesh shall consume away while they stand upon their feet, and their eyes shall consume away in their holes, and their tongue shall consume away in their mouth ... a great tumult from the Lord shall be among them; and they shall lay hold every one on the hand of his neighbor.... And Judah also shall fight at Jerusalem.... And it shall come to pass, that every one that is left of all the nations which came against Jerusalem shall go up from year to year to worship the King, the Lord of hosts, and to keep the feast of tabernacles" (Zech 14:1-21).

21. *Malachi:* "Behold, he shall come, saith the Lord of hosts. But who may abide in the day of his coming? and who shall stand when he appeareth? for he is like a refiner's fire, and like fuller's soap ... he will purify the sons of Levi, and purge them as gold and silver" (Mal 3:1-5); "Behold, I will send you Elijah the prophet before the coming of the great and dreadful day of the Lord. And he shall turn the heart of the fathers to the children, and the heart of the children to the fathers, lest I come and smite the earth with a curse" (Mal 4:5-6).

Testimony of 4 N. T. Prophets

1. *Jesus:* "For the Son of man shall come in the glory of his Father with his angels; and then shall he reward every man according to his works" (Mt 16:27. See also Mt 13:39-43, 49-50; 24:29-31; 25:31-46; Lk 9:26); "when the Son of man shall sit in the throne of his glory, ye also shall sit upon twelve thrones, judging the twelve tribes of Israel" (Mt 19:28; Lk 22:29-30); "Behold, your house is left unto you desolate . . . ye shall not see me henceforth, till ye shall say, Blessed is he that cometh in the name of the Lord" (Mt 23:37-39; Lk 13:34-35); "For as lightning cometh out of the east, and shineth even unto the west; so shall also the coming of the Son of man be. For wheresoever the carcass is, there will be eagles be gathered together" (Mt 24:27-28); "Immediately after the tribulation of those days (from the abomination of desolation to the second advent, Mt 24:15-31) shall the sun be darkened, and the moon shall not give her light, and the stars shall fall from heaven, and the powers of the heavens shall be shaken; *and then* shall appear the sign of the Son of man in heaven; *and then* shall all the tribes of the earth mourn, and they shall see the Son of man coming in the clouds of heaven with power and great glory; and he shall send his angels with a great sound of a trumpet, and they shall gather together his elect from the four winds, from one end of the earth to the other" (Mt 24:29-31); "But as the days of Noe (Noah) were, so shall also the coming of the Son of man be . . . they were eating and drinking, marrying and giving in marriage, until the day that Noe entered into the ark, and knew not until the flood came, and *took them all away;* so shall also the coming of the Son of man be" (Mt 24:37-44. See also Lk 17:22-37); "When the Son of man shall come in his glory, and all the holy angels with him, *then* shall he sit upon the throne of his glory: and before him shall be gathered all nations: and he shall separate them one from another, as a shepherd divideth his sheep from the goats. *Then* shall the King say unto them on his right hand, Come, ye blessed of my Father, inherit the kingdom prepared for you. . . . *Then* shall he say also unto them on his left hand, Depart from me, ye cursed, into everlasting fire, prepared for the devil and his angels. And these shall go away into everlasting punishment; but the righteous into life eternal" (Mt 25:31-46); "Hereafter shall ye see the Son of man sitting on the right hand of power, and coming in the clouds of heaven" (Mt 26:64; Mk 14:62); "And there shall be signs in the sun, and in the moon, and in the stars; and upon the earth distress of nations, with perplexity; the sea and the waves roaring; men's hearts failing them for fear, and for looking after those things which are coming on the earth: for the powers of heaven shall be shaken. *And then* shall they see the Son of man coming in a cloud with power and great glory" (Lk 21:25-28).

2. *Peter:* "And he shall send Jesus Christ, which before was preached unto you; whom the heaven must receive until the times of the restitution of all things, which God hath spoken by the mouth of all his holy prophets since the world began" (Acts 3:20-21); "After this (after the church age) I will return, and will build again the tabernacle (kingdom) of David" (Acts 15:13-18; Amos 9:11-12; Isa 9:6-7; Jer 30:9; Ezek 34:23; 37:24; Hos 3:5).

3. *Paul:* "Blindness in part is happened to Israel, until the fullness of the Gentiles be come in. And so all Israel shall be saved: as it is written, There shall come out of Sion the deliverer, and shall turn away ungodliness from Jacob" (Rom 11:25-27); "And to you who are troubled rest with us, when the Lord Jesus shall be revealed from heaven with his mighty angels, in flaming fire taking vengeance on them that know not God, and that obey not the gospel of our Lord Jesus Christ. . . . When he comes to be glorified in His saints" (2 Th 1:7-10); "*And then* shall that Wicked be revealed, whom the Lord shall consume with the spirit of his mouth, and shall destroy with the brightness of his coming" (2 Th 2:8); "Looking for that blessed hope, and the glorious appearing of the great God and our Saviour Jesus Christ" (Tit 2:13); "unto them that look for him shall he appear the second time" (Heb 9:28).

4. *John:* "Behold, he cometh with clouds, and every eye shall see him, and they also which pierced him; and all the kindreds of the earth shall wail because of him" (Rev 1:7); "I saw heaven opened, and behold a white horse; and he that sat upon him was called Faithful and True, and in righteousness he doth judge and make war . . . the armies which were in heaven followed him on white horses, clothed in linen, white and clean. . . . And I saw the beast, and the kings of the earth, and their armies, gathered together to make war against him that sat on his horse, and against his army. And the beast was taken, and with him the false prophet that wrought miracles before him, with which he deceived them that had received the mark of the beast, and them that worshipped his image. These both were cast alive into the lake of fire burning with brimstone" (Rev 19:11-21).

The Testimony of Angels

"He shall be great, and shall be called the Son of the Highest: and the Lord God shall give unto him the throne of his father David: and he shall reign over the house of Jacob for ever; and of his kingdom there shall be no end" (Lk 1:32-33); "Ye men of Galilee, why stand ye gazing up into heaven? This same Jesus, which is taken up from you into heaven, shall so come in like manner as ye have seen him go into heaven" (Acts 1:11).

Testimony of the Lord's Prayer

"Thy kingdom come. Thy will be done in earth, as it is in heaven" (Mt 6:10). Realizing that "he must reign, till he hath put all enemies under his feet" see also 1 Cor 15:24-28; Rev 11:15; 19:11-21; Dan 2:44-45; 7:9-14, 27; Isa 9:6-7; Zech 14; Jude 14-15; 2 Th 1:7-10.

Testimony of the Lord's Supper

"For as often as ye do eat this bread, and drink this cup, ye do show the Lord's death TILL HE COME" (1 Cor 11:26).

3. *The First and Second Comings of God the Father to the Earth*

Besides the two comings of Christ, the Bible also teaches a first and second coming of God the Father to the earth in connection with future events:

(1) God the Father will accompany Christ to the earth at His second advent. He will then give the kingdoms of this world to Jesus Christ, His Son, to rule, after which He will return to heaven to await the putting down of all His enemies by His Son in the Millennium (1 Cor 15:24-28; Eph 1:10). That God the Father comes visibly to the earth with Christ at the second advent is stated in Zech 14:5 and other scriptures. See Dan 2:44-45; 7:9-14; Mt 16:27-28; 25:31-46; Tit 2:13. Joel 2:11 says that God will utter His voice before His army, at Armageddon, so it will be a definite visible appearing of God the Father to men at that time — the second advent of Christ.

(2) The second time in the future, definitely known to us as a time when God the Father will come to the earth, is after the second advent of Christ and the Millennium, when He moves His capital city, the New Jerusalem, from the planet heaven to the planet earth, thereafter to live among men for ever (Rev 21-22; Heb 11:10-16; 12:2-23; 13:14).

4. *Time of the Second Coming of Christ*

Because some have foolishly set dates for the second advent of Christ, dates from 1843 A.D. to the present year, it does not eliminate the fact that He will come in due time. The predicting of the exact year continues, being changed from time to time as failure of fulfillment happens and scholars change their theories. Jesus warned against all this and declared that neither He, Himself, nor the angels knew of that time (Mk 13:32; Acts 1:7). See Mt 24:32-51; 25:13.

Although we cannot know the day or the hour we can know that it will be a pre-millennial second coming to the earth, that is, Christ will come before His 1,000-year reign on earth (Rev 20:4-10).

From the many scripture quotations above we can see that the prophets believed in a literal, visible return of Christ to the earth. The church also believed this for the first two centuries, but in the third century there arose a school of interpreters under Origen who began to teach that the Bible was only a spiritual and symbolic book. They ceased to believe in the literal advent of Christ to the earth.

When Constantine was converted and the Roman Empire became nominally Christian, it appeared to the church world that the Millennium had come and that Christ was already reigning on the earth. Then the church in union with the world plunged into the dark ages until there was an awakening by the Reformers of the 16th century, leaders who began to restore the plain literal meaning of Scripture — and today the trend is toward a literal return and an earthly reign of Christ on earth.

Sometime, about the year 1700 A.D., the theory of post-millennialism began to be taught — the theory that the church will prosper until the world is converted, and this triumph of the church will be the Millennium. Some today teach and believe this while there are others who teach that there will not be a Millennium. But Scripture teaches plainly that there will be a Millennium between the second advent and the new earth (Rev 20:1-10; 21:1-22:5).

5. *There are 12 reasons for a Pre-millennial Second Advent:*

(1) The Antichrist, whose coming all agree will be pre-millennial, is to be destroyed with the brightness of Christ's second coming (2 Th 2:7-8; Rev 19:11-21).

(2) The second coming of Christ to reign on the earth is "immediately after the tribulation" (Mt 24:29-31). And, the tribulation is just before the Millennium (Mt 24:15-22, 29:31; Rev 6:1-19:21).

(3) There is to be a separation of the wheat and the tares and this will take place just before the establishment of the kingdom as is clear from Mt 13:40-43.

(4) The conditions of the days of Lot and Noah will exist in the days immediately before the second advent (Mt 24:37-42; Lk 17:22-37; 1 Tim 4; 2 Tim 3-4; 2 Pet 3). This certainly does not teach a converted world before Christ comes.

(5) The millennial kingdom is to be a literal one, as much so as any other of this world (Isa 9:6-7; Dan 2:44-45; 7:9-14, 18, 22, 27; Zech 14; Rev 11:15; 20:4-6).

(6) The resurrections prove a pre-millennial coming of Christ to rule men on earth. The righteous dead will be raised before the Millennium, for they are to reign with Christ during that time (Rev 20:4-6). The wicked dead will not be resurrected until at the end of the Millennium (Rev 20:11-15).

(7) Whenever Christ comes to earth Satan will be bound. And since he is to remain bound throughout the time of the Millennium to be loosed at the end of that time, then there can be no Millennium until the second advent of Christ (Rev 20).

(8) Israel will be restored and regathered when Christ comes to earth (Mt 24:31) and, since they are fully restored during the Millennium, Christ must first come before the Millennium begins. See fallacy 5, Chapter 9.

(9) The Millennium will be the last 1,000 years before the new earth period wherein there will be eternal righteousness without any enemies left on earth (2 Pet 3:13; Rev 21-22). To accomplish this and rid the earth of all sin Christ will need to reign during this 1,000-year period — the Millennium (1 Cor 15:24-28). His coming to earth or the second advent will therefore take place before the Millennium.

(10) The greatest tribulation and martyrdom of saints that ever has been or ever will be will continue up to the very time that Christ comes to reign and rid the earth of all such troubles (Mt 24:15-22, 29-31; Rev 6:1-19:21).

(11) When Jesus taught His disciples that they would "sit upon twelve thrones, judging the twelve tribes of Israel" He referred to the Millennial kingdom which could not be set up until He would return in glory (Mt 19:28; 25:31-46).

(12) The apostles taught that the kingdom would not be set up until the second advent (Acts 3:19-21; 15:13-18; Rom 11:25-29; 2 Th 2; 2 Tim 4:1; Jude 14-15; Rev 11:15; 19:11-21).

6. *The 10-fold manner of the Second Advent:*

(1) "As the lightning cometh out of the east, and shineth even unto the west, so shall also the coming of the Son of man be" (Mt 24:27).

(2) He will come as a great destruction to the ungodly, as did the flood of Noah (Mt 23:37-51; 25:31-46; 1 Th 5:2; 2 Th 1:7-10; 2:8; Jude 14-15; Zech 14; Isa 43:1-4; 65:1-5).

(3) Christ will come visibly as He went away (Acts 1:11; Rev 1:7; Mt 25:29-31).

(4) He will come in brightness and fire (2 Th 7-10; 2:8; Ezek 38:17-21; Mal 4:1-6).

(5) He will come in vengeance and wrath (Rev 14:14-20; 19:11-21; Jude 14-15; 2 Th 1:7-10).

(6) He will come with great power and glory (Mt 16:27; 24:29-31; 25:31-46).

(7) He will come with the raptured saints and His angels from heaven (Rev 19:11-21; Zech 14:5; 2 Th 1:7-10; Jude 14-15; Mt 24:29-31).

(8) His coming will be with clouds (Rev 1:7; Dan 7:13-14; Mt 24:27-31; 26:64).

(9) He is coming as both Judge and King (Mt 25:31-46; Dan 7:9-14; Rev 19:11-21).

(10) He is coming as a thief in the night (1 Th 5:2-4; 2 Pet 3:10; Rev 16:15).

7. *The 20-fold purpose of the Second Advent:*

(1) Judge the living nations (Mt 25:31-46; Dan 7:9-14).

(2) Establish true worship (Ps 72:11; Zech 14:16-21; 2 Th 1:10).

(3) Bring salvation (Isa 49:6; Rom 11:25-29).

(4) Destroy enemies (Jude 14-15; 2 Th 2:7-8; Rev 19:11-21; Joel 2-3; Zech 14).

(5) Deliver creation from bondage (Rom 8:21-24; Isa 11:1-11; 35:1-8; 65:20-25).

(6) Re-establish David's throne and kingdom (Isa 9:6-7; Jer 30:7-11; Ezek 36:1-37:26; Hos 3:5; Lk 1:32-33; Acts 15:13-18).

(7) Execute righteousness and justice on earth (Isa 11:3-9; Jer 23:5-6).

(8) Reign over all nations (Dan 2:44-45; 7:9-14; Zech 14; Rev 11:15; 19:11-21).

(9) Establish the raptured saints as kings and priests (Mt 19:28; Rev 2:26-27; 5:10; 20:4-6; Dan 7:18, 22, 27; 1 Cor 6).

(10) Regather all Israel completely (Gen 49:10; Isa 11:11-12; Mt 24:31). See fallacy 5, Chapter 9.

(11) Put down all rebellion on earth (1 Cor 15:24-28; Rev 2:27).

(12) Build the Jewish Millennial temple (Ezek 43:7; Zech 6:12-13).

(13) Establish God's glory on earth (Isa 4; 40:5; Ezek 39:21; Mt 16:27; 25:31).

(14) Remove every curse from the earth (Isa 35; 65:20-25; Mic 4; 1 Cor 15:24-28; Rev 21:1-7; 22:3).

(15) Bring universal peace and prosperity (Isa 2:2-4; Mic 4:1-7).

(16) End the times of the Gentiles (Zech 14; Lk 21:24; Rom 11:25-29; Rev 11:1-2; 19:11-21).

(17) Possess the earth (Ps 2; Rev 11:15; Zech 14; Rev 20).

(18) Build up Zion (Ps 102:16; Ezek 48).

(19) Establish Jerusalem as the capital of the world (Ezek 40:5-48:35; Isa 62:7; 65:18-19; Jer 3:17; Joel 3:20; Zech 14).

(20) Establish an eternal sinless earthly program (Gen 8:22; 9:12; 17:8; Isa 9:6-7; 59:20-21; Ezek 37:25; Dan 2:44-45; 7:9-14, 18, 22, 27; Zech 14:1-5; Lk 1:32-33; 1 Cor 15:24-28; Rev 11:15; 22:4-5).

8. *There are 25 incentives of the Rapture and Second Advent:*

These two great doctrines are incentives to a godly and practical life of holiness in this present world. *They are incentives to:*

(1) Watchfulness (Mt 24:37-45; 25:13; Rev 16:15).
(2) Readiness for heaven (Mt 24:43-44).
(3) Faithfulness to God (Mt 24:45-51).
(4) Diligence in Christian living (Mt 25:14-30).
(5) Sobriety — soberness (1 Th 5:1-11; 1 Pet 1:13; 4:7; 5:8).
(6) Moderation unto all men (Phil 4:5).
(7) Repentance (Acts 3:19-21; Rev 3:3).
(8) Being unashamed of Christ and His words (Mk 8:38).
(9) Salvation (Mk 16:24-27; Heb 9:28).
(10) Patience (Heb 10:36-39; Jas 5:7-8).
(11) Mortification of the flesh (Col 3:3-10; Rom 8:12-13).
(12) Sincerity and uprightness (Phil 1:10).
(13) Sanctification and purity (1 Th 5:23; 1 Jn 3:1-3).
(14) Ministerial faithfulness (2 Tim 4:1-2; 1 Pet 5:2-4).
(15) Development in virtues (2 Pet 1:4-11).
(16) Obedience (1 Tim 6:13; Rom 1:5; 16:26).
(17) Holiness and godliness (2 Pet 3:11-13; Phil 3:21).
(18) Brotherly love (1 Th 3:1-13; 1 Cor 13).
(19) Love and hope of His appearing (2 Tim 4:8; Tit 2:13).
(20) Denial of ungodliness and worldly lusts (Tit 2:11-14).
(21) Pursue and lay hold of eternal life (Mt 19:27-29; Rom 2:7).
(22) Blamelessness (1 Cor 1:7-8; Eph 1:1-4).
(23) Purity of life and conduct (1 Jn 3:1-3).
(24) Growth in grace (2 Pet 3:18).
(25) Constant alertness against falling (2 Pet 2:17; Heb 14:15).

Chapter 9
37 Fallacies
concerning the Rapture and Second Advent:

FALLACY 1: The word "rapture" is not found in the Bible, therefore, it is not a biblical docrine. Man is not going to heaven after all.

TRUTH: As to men going to heaven some day, this is taught in many scriptures (Jn 14:1-3; Eph 3:15; Heb 9:27; 12:22-23; 1 Pet 3:22; Rev 1:1; 5:8-10; 12:5; 14:1-5; 15:1-4; 19:1-10). At least two men are even now in heaven in their mortal bodies (Gen 5:24; Zech 4:14; Rev 11:3-12).

As to the word "rapture" not being in the Bible, this does not prevent it from being a truly biblical doctrine. The words "receive you unto myself" (Jn 14:1-3) and "caught up to meet the Lord in the air" (1 Th 4:13-18) and other terms meaning the same as the word "rapture" are found in the Bible. See many proofs of a rapture in Chapter 7.

The words Bible, demon, omnipresent, omniscience, Adamite, ambition, animal, anarchy, agriculture, astronomy, apostasy, botony, criticism, manufacture, and many other words are not found in the Bible text, but all true Bible students recognize such words as being biblical as far as truth is concerned.

FALLACY 2: The Gr. word "parousia" is used only of the second advent of Christ — it is never used of another coming of the Lord called "the rapture."

TRUTH: The word "parousia" is not used exclusively of the second advent. It literally means personal appearance, personal presence, and personal coming into the presence of another person.

6 ways "parousia" is used in the N. T.

(1) Of Paul's bodily presence before other men (2 Cor 10:10; Phil 2:12).

(2) Of the bodily presence of other men coming before Paul (1 Cor 16:17; 2 Cor 7:6-7).

(3) Of the coming of a certain day (2 Pet 3:12).

(4) Of the appearance and coming together of men and Christ — in their bodily presence in meeting each other in the rapture, or in the air before the tribulation (Lk 21:34-36; 1 Cor 15:23; 1 Th 2:19-20; 3:13; 4:13; 5:23; 2 Th 2:1; Jas 5:7-8; 2 Pet 1:16; 1 Jn 2:28; Zech 14:5; Jude 14-15; Rev 19:1-21).

(5) Of the visible and bodily presence of Christ and all the raptured saints coming to the earth to meet men and to live with them in person (Mt 24:3, 27, 37, 39; 2 Th 2:7-8; 2 Pet 3:4; Rev 1:7; 11:18; 19:1-21; Ezek 43:7).

(6) Of the coming of Antichrist in person with power from Satan to do miracles in his efforts to deceive the world (2 Th 2:9).

It is just as much a parousia to meet Christ in the air as it is to meet Him on earth. It does not matter who meets whom and when or how, for any bodily or personal meeting of two or more persons is a *parousia.*

Parousia is not the only Gr. word used of the rapture and the second advent. There are four others used of these two distinct comings, as follows:

(1) *Phaneros*, to shine, be apparent, be manifest, be seen, or to appear bodily to someone. It is translated *appear* regarding the rapture in Col 3:4; 1 Pet 5:4; 1 Jn 2:28; 3:2.

(2) *Erchnomai*, to come. It is used of the rapture in 1 Cor 15:35; Jn 21:23; and of the second advent in Mt 24:30, 42, 43; 25:13, 21; Acts 1:11; Rev. 1:7. Both are comings of the Lord.

(3) *Epiphania*, appearance, brightness, It is used of the rapture in 1 Tim 6:14; 2 Tim 4:1, 8; Tit 2:13; and of the second advent in 2 Th 2:8 when Christ appears to destroy Antichrist.

(4) *Apokalupsis,* revelation, unveiling, becoming visible. It is used of the rapture when Christ is revealed to His saints in 1 Cor 1:7; 1 Pet 1:7, and of the second advent in 2 Th 1:7-10 when He is revealed to the world of men with His saints.

It matters not which word we use of either coming — the rapture or the second advent — the words simply mean coming, personal presence, appearance, visible sight, and revelation. Any coming of one person to another is, in the usage of all these words, a coming. And so, to use *parousia* to disprove a rapture and to prove a second advent only, is pointless because the word is used of both comings which take place at least 7 years apart with the end of these comings being entirely different as to time, place, and purpose.

FALLACY 3: There is only one future coming of Christ from heaven, not two.

TRUTH: There are two separate and distinct comings of Christ out of heaven in the future that we can call a *coming* of the Lord. One is from heaven before the tribulation when He comes from heaven and out of heaven to the clouds surrounding the earth to rapture all the dead and living in Christ. He will then take them to heaven to live with Him and His Father and all others who dwell in heaven (Jn 14:1-3; Lk 21:34-36; 1 Cor 15:23, 51-54; Eph 5:27; Phil 3:21; 1 Th 4:13-18; 5:1-11; 2 Th 2:7-8; Col 3:4; Jas 5:7-8; 1 Jn 3:1-3). Another coming, and this also will be from heaven, is the second advent to the earth — and not to the clouds only — to bring all the raptured saints from heaven with Him to fight at Armageddon and set up a kingdom in the world (Zech 14:5; Mt 24:29-31; 2 Th 1:7-10; Jude 14-15; Rev 19:11-21).

FALLACY 4: The rapture is a secret coming.

TRUTH: The Bible does not say one word about the rapture being a secret meeting, or that God will steal away the saints like a thief. The rapture is to be an event that is noisy enough to be announced by a shout and the voice of an archangel, and with the trump of God, Himself (1 Th 4:16; 1 Cor 15:51-54). And, it will be over in the twinkling of an eye (1 Cor 15:51-52). Even if it could be classed as secret, it will not last very long. As to the second advent it is not to be secret either, but it will be sudden like a thief coming to rob (Mt 24:43; Lk 12:33-39; 1 Th 5:2-14; 2 Pet 3:10; Rev 16:15).

FALLACY 5: Jesus said that the church would be raptured immediately after the tribulation (Mt 24:29-31). The *elect* of Mt 24:31 is the church.

TRUTH: Jesus said nothing about the church being raptured immediately after the tribulation. No person will be raptured at that time, for all who go to heaven in the raptures will have been raptured by then, and will have already eaten the marriage supper there before the second advent begins (Rev 19:1-21). These saints will accompany Christ from heaven as stated in Rev 19:14 and in Jude 14-15; Zech 14:5. The *elect* referred to in Mt 24:29-21 is the Jewish elect that will be on earth while the church and all other raptured saints will be in heaven. How could the church be in heaven up to the time of the second advent and still be down on earth waiting for the second advent to take place? This would be impossible. This elect − the Jewish elect − is the one that will flee from Judea into the mountains (Mt 24:15-22). To say that the elect of Mt 24:31 is the church would be saying that all who make up the church will need to move to Judea before Antichrist sets up the abomination of desolation in the Jewish temple, for whoever is the elect at that time will flee from Judea into the mountains (Mt 24:15-22). In such a case Judea would be extremely overpopulated, with all the present nation of Israel therein, besides all the people from all other lands who make up the church, living there at the same time.

We have no prediction of the church being gathered together in Judea at the end time but we have scores of passages repeatedly using the words *gather, gathered,* and *gathering,* which foretell of the final gathering of Israel in that place. Those who have taken part in the partial re-gathering before the second advent will be the *elect* of Mt 24:15-22 who will flee into the mountains when Antichrist sets up the abomination of desolation.

4 main Elects of Scripture

(1) The Messiah (Isa 42:1; 1 Pet 2:6).
(2) Israel (Isa 45:4; 65:9, 22; 1 Pet 1:2; 2 Tim 2:20).

(3) The church (Col 3:12; Tit 1:1; Eph 1:4; 2:10).

(4) Faithful angels (1 Tim 5:21).

8 great Gatherings of men — historical and prophetical

(1) The first great gathering of Israel, God's elect, in the days of Ezra and Nehemiah after the first great captivity of all Israel to Assyria (2 Ki 17) and to Babylon (2 Ki 25). *Historical.*

(2) The rapture of Christ, some of the O. T. saints who were resurrected then (Mt 27:52-53), and the souls and spirits of O. T. saints whose bodies were not resurrected. All were captured by Christ and taken to heaven with Him when He ascended on high (Mt 12:40; Eph 4:8-10; Heb 2:14-15). *Historical.*

(3) The second re-gathering of Jews to make a great nation in our day (Isa 11:11-12; Ezek 37). Partially fulfilled, and will continue in fulfillment until the second advent of Christ. *Historical and prophetical.*

For scriptures on the complete and final re-gathering of Israel see the following: Mt 24:31; Gen 49:10; Lev 26:40-45; Dt 4:25-31; 30:1-10; 31:28-30; Ps 102:16-22; Isa 10:21; 11:11-12; 14:1-8; 27:12-13; 43:5-7; 44:1-5, 21-23; 45:14-17; 56:8; 60:8-22; 65:18-25; 66:18-21; Jer 3:14-25; 7:1-7; 16:14-21; 23:3-8; 24:5-7; 30:1-24; 31:1-40; 32:37-44; 33:6-26; 46:26-28; 50:19-20; Ezek 11:17-21; 16:60-63; 20:33-38; 28:25-26; 34:11-31; 36:22-38; Ezek 37; Hos 1:10-11; 2:14-23; 3:5, Joel 3; Amos 9:11-15; Mic 2:12-13; 4:1-13; 5:3-15; Zeph 2:6-15; 3:8-20; Zech 8:7-8, 23; 10:9-12; Acts 15:13-18.

(4) Rapture of the church and O. T. saints before the tribulation (Jn 14:1-3; Lk 21:34-36; 1 Cor 15:23, 51-56; Phil 3:21; Col 3:4; Eph 5:27; 1 Th 2:19-20; 3:13; 4:13-18; 5:1-11, 23; Jas 5:7-8; Rev 5:8-10; 19:1-10). See Chapter 10. *Prophetical.*

(5) The rapture of 144,000 Jews (Rev 7:1-8; 9:14; 12:5; 14:1-5). *Prophetical.*

(6) The rapture of tribulation saints to heaven (Rev 6:9-11; 7:9-17; 14:12-13; 15:1-4; 20:4-7). *Prophetical.*

(7) The gathering of the living nations to judgment to Jerusalem (Mt 25:31-46; Dan 7:9-14; 11:45). *Prophetical.*

(8) The final gathering of nations against Christ and God at Jerusalem (Rev 20:7-10). *Prophetical.*

FALLACY 6: God's purpose for the church is to take them through the tribulation before the rapture—to protect saints from death as He protected Noah in the flood, Daniel in the lion's den, the Hebrews in the furnace of fire, and Israel from the plagues of Egypt. Having kept these from harm why should He change His pattern of protecting people during the tribulation? Jesus promised that He would keep the disciples from evil (Jn 17:15). God promised to keep saints from all evil even in O. T. times (Isa 43:2; Ps 91), so why should He not protect them from the terrible events of the seals, trumpets, and vials in the future tribulation?

TRUTH: This is mere childish reasoning. Informed grown-ups know that saints have been killed in all O. T. and N. T. ages (Mt 23:37-39; Heb 11:37; Acts 7:57-60; 12:2; etc.). Who among us has not heard of martyrs in all ages? One reading of Rev 6:9-11; 7:9-17; 14:9-14; 15:1-5; 20:4-6 is sufficient to disprove the above theory, for the passages show us that millions of saints in the tribulation to come, will die. Let us remember though, that the saints of the tribulation period will be people who have become saints after the rapture of the church — people who have missed the rapture and now, many of those living in the particular kingdom of the Antichrist, the old Roman Empire territory, will have a price to pay. Only the 144,000 Jews have been promised protection from the plagues of the tribulation days in Antichrist's kingdom (Rev 7:1-8; 9:4; 12:5; 14:1-5).

God does not plan to destroy saints by His wrath that will be poured out during the tribulation, but we must understand that those who will be living in the Antichrist's kingdom during the time of such wrath can expect to suffer some effects of the judgments, wars, famines, pestilences, earthquakes, plagues and woes of the seals, trumpets, and vials taking place at that time (Rev 6:1-16:21).

FALLACY 7: No man will be saved after the rapture.

TRUTH: Contrary to the above, the Bible reveals that the greatest of all spiritual revivals will take place after the rapture and during the tribulation time: "I will pour out of my Spirit upon all flesh; and your sons and daughters shall prophesy. . . . And I will show wonders in heaven above, and signs in the earth beneath; blood, and fire, and vapour of smoke: the sun shall be turned into darkness, and the moon into blood, before that great and notable day of the Lord come (the second advent); and it shall come to pass THAT WHOSOEVER SHALL CALL ON THE NAME OF THE LORD SHALL BE SAVED" (Acts 2:16-21). Multitudes will be saved and martyred in the great tribulation period (Rev 7:8-17; 12:17; Mal 4:5-6; Zech 12:10-13:1; Rom 11:25-29). This is proof that the Holy Spirit will never be taken from the world — as Jesus promised, "he may abide with you forever" (Jn 14:16).

FALLACY 8: There will be only one rapture of saints from earth to heaven.

TRUTH: There have already been 6 historical raptures to heaven, and there will be 4 more raptures to heaven, prophetical raptures, making altogether 10 separate raptures of the past and the future, as follows:

10 Historical and Prophetical Raptures:

(6 historical raptures)

(1) The rapture of Enoch about 5,145 years ago (Gen 5:24; Zech 4:14; Heb 11:4; Rev 11:2-12).

(2) The rapture of Elijah about 3,500 years ago (2 Ki 2:11; Zech 4:14; Mal 4:5-6; Rev 11:3-12).

(3) The rapture of Christ when He went to heaven and back in one day (Jn 20:17-20).

(4) The rapture of Christ with the "many" O. T. saints, and all the souls and spirits of O. T. saints not yet resurrected (Mt 27:52-53; Eph 4:8-10; 1 Cor 15:20-23; Heb 2:14-15; Ps 68:8; Acts 1:11).

(5) The rapture of Paul to the third heaven (2 Cor 12:1-4).

(6) The rapture of John to heaven (Rev 4:1-5:14).

(4 prophetical raptures)

(7) The next, a general rapture of all the dead and living in Christ of all ages up to this point: "They that are Christ's at his coming" (1 Cor 15:23, 51-54; Lk 21:34-36; Jn 14:1-3; 1 Th 2:19-20; 3:13; 4:13-18; 5:1-11, 23; 2 Th 2:7-8; Eph 5:27; Col 3:4; Phil 3:21; Tit 2:13; Jas 5:7-8; 1 Pet 1:7-12; 4:13; 2 Pet 1:11; 1 Jn 2:28; 3:2; Rev 5:8-10; 19:1-10). This rapture will be before the tribulation (see Chapters 10-12).

(8) The rapture of the 144,000 Jews to heaven (Rev 7:1-8; 9:4; 12:5; 14:1-5; 19:1-10; Isa 66:7-8; Dan 12:1). This will be in the middle of the Week (see Chapter 12).

(9) The rapture of all the tribulation martyrs of Daniel's 70th week, persons who become saved and martyred in the time between the rapture of the church and the second advent (Rev 6:9-11; 7:9-17; 13:7; 14:9-13; 15:1-4; 16:2; 17:6; 19:1-10; 20:4-6).

(10) The rapture of the two witnesses to heaven (Rev 11:3-12; 19:1-10).

FALLACY 9: "Saints" will be here on earth all through the tribulation which proves that the church will be here all that time.

TRUTH: That there will be saints on the earth during all the tribulation period is clear in many scriptures (Dan 7:21, 25; Rev 13:7; 17:6). There have been saints on earth in every generation since Adam's time — when Abel lived. But being called "saints" does not prove any group to be part of the N. T. church, which will have been raptured by this time. The 144,000 and the tribulation saints are those who will become saved after the rapture of the church (Acts 2:16-21; Rev 6:9-11; 7:1-17; 9:4; 12:5; 13:7; 14:1-5, 9-13; 15:1-4, 20:4-6). and their presence on earth then does not prove that the church is to be here in the tribulation period.

FALLACY 10: The rapture takes place at the 7th trumpet of Rev 11:15, and this is the same as the last trumpet of 1 Cor 15:51-54.

TRUTH: There is not the least relationship or similarity in these two scriptures. On the contrary, they could not possibly refer to the same event, because:

1. The trumpet of Rev 11:15 is that of an ordinary angel (Rev 8:2), while the one in 1 Cor 15:51-54 and 1 Th 4:13-18 is the trumpet of God.

2. The trumpet in Rev 11:15 is to announce a great woe upon men (Rev 8:13; 10:7-8; 11:14; 12:7-12), while the one in 1 Cor 15:52 and 1 Th 4:16 will announce a great blessing — the resurrection of the dead.

3. The trumpet of Rev 11:15 will be blown at least 3½ years after the rapture and 3½ years before the second advent, whereas the trumpet of 1 Cor and 1 Th will be blown at least 3½ years before the 7th trumpet of Rev 11:15 and at least 7 years before the second advent. Proof of this is that every detail of Rev 4:1-22:5 must be fulfilled AFTER THE CHURCHES (Rev 1:19; 4:1; Chapter 10, proof 2). The trumpet of Rev 11:15 is a "middle of the Week" detail that must happen after the rapture of the church and before any of Rev 4:1-22:5 begins to be fulfilled. One trumpet appears in the middle of these things WHICH MUST BE AFTER THE CHURCHES and the other must be blown before any of these details begin.

4. The trumpet of 1 Cor and 1 Th will herald an event that will take place "in a moment" (1 Cor 15:51-54), whereas the 7th trumpet of Revelation will herald an event that will be "days" in duration (Rev 10:7-8).

It may also be stated here that the "last" trump of 1 Cor 15:51-53 is not the last trumpet that will ever blow, as some teach, for years later at Armageddon and at the second advent trumpets will blow (Mt 24:31; Joel 2:15; Zeph 1:16; Zech 9:14). Furthermore, others will sound at all the feasts of trumpets and at other events eternally (Ezek 45:17-25; 46:14).

FALLACY 11: Jesus said that the wicked would be gathered and destroyed before the saints would be raptured (Mt 13:24-43; 24:40-45).

TRUTH: Jesus did not refer to the rapture of the church to heaven, in the above passages. In Mt 13 He simply revealed that there would be some wicked and some righteous in the same world until the end of this age — even up to the second advent, itself. After Armageddon there will be a gathering of both the righteous and the wicked to determine who will be worthy of entering the Millennium (Mt 25:31-46). There is no rapture referred to here at all, either in Mt 13 or Mt 25, for all the raptures of all the saints will be over by then and the raptured ones will be living in their mansions in heaven

(Jn 14:1-3). Then, finally, after the marriage supper of the Lamb in heaven they will leave heaven with Christ, on white horses, accompanying Him to the earth to fight at Armageddon (Rev 19:1-21). The purpose of the separation and gathering referred to then, is to decide on who will continue to live on earth in the Millennial kingdom, not who will go in a rapture that has, by this time, been over for several years.

FALLACY 12: Scripture does not say that there will be at least 7 years between the rapture and the second advent of Christ.

TRUTH: Scripture plainly teaches that there will be at least 7 years between the rapture and the second advent, as shown in the following:

1. The time element of Rev 4:1 through 19:21 is 7 years, especially from the first seal of Rev 6:1-2 to the 7th vial of Rev 16:17-21. In Rev 6:1-2 we have the rise of the Antichrist from Syria after the 10 kingdoms are formed inside the old Roman Empire territory (Dan 7:7-8, 19-25). In Dan 9:27 it is revealed that he will make a 7-year covenant with Israel, and we know that this contract will be made when he begins to conquer the 10 kingdoms, overthrowing 3 of the 10 in the first 3½ years of the tribulation period (Dan 7:7-8, 23-24; Rev 13:5; 17:8-17). He then turns on Israel and defeating them in battle, drives them out of their country (Dan 11:40-43; Mt 24:15-22). This time is called "in the midst of the week" when he breaks his contract with Israel and determines to destroy them (Dan 9:27; Mt 24:15-22). This is 3½ years before he is destroyed at Armageddon (Dan 7:21, 25; 12:1-7; Rev 11:1-3; 12:6, 14; 13-5).

2. The teaching of 2 Th 2:7-8 is that the hinderer of lawlessness is taken out of the world before Antichrist comes. And, the hinderer being taken out is definitely the rapture of the church, as proved in Chapter 10, proof 1, below. Since the church is raptured before the revelation of Antichrist, who is here for 7 years, then it is clear that there will be at least 7 years between the rapture and the second advent.

3. It being true that every detail of Rev 4:1-22:5 MUST BE AFTER THE CHURCHES, as proved in Chapter 10, proof 2 below, and the time element of these happenings, which include the reign of Antichrist, being 7 years as shown above, then the conclusion is that there are at least 7 years of time between the rapture and the second advent. The only time element we do not have any scripture for is: how much sooner than the beginning of the 7-year tribulation period will the rapture take place, if indeed it is to happen sometime sooner than that period. We do have, however, various scriptures that indicate we should be looking for the rapture to take place at any time (1 Cor 1:7; Phil 3:21; 1 Th 1:10; Tit 2:13).

FALLACY 13: The church is not ready to meet the Lord, so it will have to face the Antichrist and the refining fires of the tribulation in order to purify it and make it ready for the rapture.

TRUTH: This fallacy is not only unscriptural but also ridiculous when we agree that "there is no respect of persons with God" (Rom 2:11) and to be fair to all alike would require Him to bring back all the O. T. saints and those of the church who are now dead, everyone from every past generation expected to be caught up with the living saints in the rapture — to bring them back to be purified and refined in preparation for the rapture, by the Antichrist. Contrary to such a processing of all the saints by Antichrist and the tribulation — as a qualification for the rapture — we learn from 1 Th 4:16 that the all important qualification for the rapture is being "in Christ." How could facing the Antichrist bring anyone more "into Christ" and make him better qualified than believers in the past ages? Is Antichrist really necessary in God's plan of salvation? The answer is "no." Furthermore, the greater part of the world will not be ruled by Antichrist, and we have no passage of Scripture even suggesting that there will be an end-time exodus of Christians from all lands outside the Antichrist's kingdom into his empire in order for them to become refined and thus qualified to go in the rapture. The truth is that everyone *in Christ* in every generation, whether dead or alive, is qualified to go to heaven and also take part in the rapture — and this is all sufficient (1 Th 4:16; 1 Cor 15:23).

FALLACY 14: Famous churchmen agree that the church will be raptured after the tribulation — from tribulation to glory has been the universal belief of the church in all ages. In 1830 A.D. the pre-tribulation rapture teaching began and it has become popular ever since.

TRUTH: Instead of being taught by Christians for the first time in 1830 A.D., the pre-tribulation rapture was taught by Jesus, Himself, as well as Paul, Peter, Luke, James, Matthew, John, and Jude, in their writings of the N. T. which was completed in 96 A.D. It is from these original authors of the N. T. that we get our doctrine of the rapture of the church before the tribulation. And, to say that this doctrine was first discovered in 1830 A.D. is like saying that justification by faith was first discovered as a doctrine for the church, by Luther in 1517 A.D. The truth is that both these doctrines were discovered when the Bible was written, and they were taught many centuries before 1517 and 1830 A.D.

FALLACY 15: Every eye shall see Christ at the rapture, as proved by Mt 24:30 and Rev 1:7.

TRUTH: Neither one of the above scriptures refers to the rapture, but both refer to the second advent when Christ will literally come to the earth *with* all the raptured saints to set up a kingdom at the end of the tribulation. At the rapture of the saints before the tribulation, not a person on earth will see Christ, but those who are caught up in the air will see Him in visible form when they join Him in the clouds (1 Th 4:13-18; Col 3:4; Jn 14:1-3). The rapture will take place in a moment (1 Cor 15:51-54) and everyone who has a part in it will see Christ at that time. As to the second advent, after it occurs, there will be an ever increasing number of persons seeing Him in visible form as He rules in His kingdom, for Isaiah said "all nations shall flow into it" (Isa 2:1-4; 52:15). See also Zech 8:23; Dan 7:9-14, 18, 27; Ezek 43:7; Rev 11:15.

FALLACY 16: The statement "he that shall endure to the end, the same shall be saved" in Mt. 24:13, proves that the church is on earth to the very end of this age.

TRUTH: The reference is not to the church, but to Israel who will be on earth up to the very end of this age and will see Christ coming from heaven with His raptured saints and angels to deliver them from Antichrist (Zech 14:1-21; Mt 24:29-31; 25:31-46; Rev 1:7; 19:11-21). Christ told Israel that they would not see Him again until the very end of the age (Mt 23:37-39), and Zechariah predicted that He would land on the mount of Olives at that time (Zech 14:4; Rev 1:7).

FALLACY 17: The statement "look up and lift up your heads; for your redemption draweth nigh" (Lk 21:28) confirms that the church is still here until the second advent, and then it is raptured and fully redeemed.

TRUTH: This again is not a reference to the church and its redemption but rather to the coming redemption of Israel at the second advent when all Israel will be redeemed or born again (Isa 66:7-8; Jer 30; Dan 9:24-27; Rom 11:25-28; Zech 12:10-13:1; Mt 23:37-39; Lk 21:25-33).

FALLACY 18: The term "the fullness of the Gentiles" refers to the completion of the number of Gentiles that will make up the church, and since this number is not complete until the second advent the church must be here throughout all the tribulation.

TRUTH: There is no scripture which says that there must be, or that there will be a certain number of people in the N. T. church before it can be raptured. The term "the fullness of the Gentiles" is the same as "the times of the Gentiles" (Lk 21:24; Rom 11:25-29). These are political and prophetical terms referring to the times in the history of Israel when the nation has been, and yet will be oppressed by the Gentiles. These "times" began in Egypt when Israel was first oppressed by Gentiles in the days of Moses. They will end at the second advent with the last oppression of the Jews by Gentiles (Lk 21:24; Rev 11:1-2; Zech 14; Ezek 38-39; Rev 19:11-21; Dan 12:1, Isa 66:7-8; Jer 30:7; Mt 24:15-22). In all, there will have been 8 great world empires oppressing Israel in the times of the Gentiles — Egypt, Assyria, Babylon, Medo-Persia, Greece, Rome, Revised Rome, and Revived Grecia (Rev 17:8-17). And since the church is not referred to at all here, it certainly would not be necessary for it to remain on earth during the tribulation when the final days of "the times of the Gentiles — Jacob's trouble" in the last 3½ years of this age are taking place.

There is no relationship between the church and the "times of the Gentiles." The church was not started until more than 1,700 years after the "times of the Gentiles" began and the church will be raptured before these "times" end.

The truth about the Times of the Gentiles

It is taught by some that "the times of the Gentiles" will be 2,520 years long, this being the time from Daniel's day to the second advent. But Daniel did not see the entire times of the Gentiles — all of the 8 world empires to oppress Israel during those times, as seen in Rev 17:8-17. He saw only that portion of the times of the Gentiles that would occur from his day forward.

The 2,520-year theory of the length of "the times of the Gentiles" is based on the "seven times" of Lev 26 where it is stated that God would punish Israel "seven times more" for her sins (Lev 26:18, 21, etc.). It is believed that a prophetic year is 360 days long, and that these 360 days really refer to 360 years, thus making a day for a year. Seven times 360 would make a total of 2,520 years on this basis. Men have set dates for an ending of these 2,520 years from 1843 A.D. to the present time, some of the more emphasized years being 1914, 1927, 1932 A.D. as well as several others. It is believed that the 2,520 years began in 606 B.C., or 616 B.C., or in some other year in Daniel's day. This accounts for the supposed ending of these "times" being set for different years. One can only stretch 2,520 years out over a period of 2,520 years and the beginning date selected determines the ending date. As time moved along in the past date setters moved their dates ahead but now they are about to run out of years with which to speculate. The above stated 2,520-year theory is completely unscriptural because:

1. The expression "seven times" is found 23 times in the O. T. and in no instance does it refer to a period of 2,520 years.

2. If the word "time" means a year of 360 days, then 360 of our 24-hour periods or days is to be understood — and not changed into 360 years. When Scripture uses a certain number of days to correspond with the same number of years, the statement thereof is clear, as in Num 14:33-34 and Ezek 4:5-6, and in such cases a day is always a day and a year is always a year. No one has any authority to change a day into a year.

3. If "seven times" meant 2,520 years in Lev 26, we would have 4 periods of 2,520 or a total of 10,080 years to account for because the passage uses the term 4 different times regarding Israel being punished further if a previously stated judgment did not cause them to "be reformed" (Lev 26:23) and if they did not "hearken unto" God (Lev 26:18, 21, 24, 28). The progression of stated judgments followed by threats of more punishment for "seven times' if reformation did not take place, begins with Lev 26:14.

4. If we had the authority to make one "seven times" of Scripture to mean 2,520 years, then by the same authority we could make every other "seven times" of the Bible to mean that many years. In such a case we would have Jacob bowing down to Esau for 2,520 years (Gen 33:3), the Jews sprinkling blood 2,520 years every time they made a sacrifice (Lev 4:6, 17; 8:11), the time for cleansing a leper as 2,520 years (Lev 14:7, 16, 27, 51), Israel marching around the walls of Jericho for 2,520 years on the 7th day (Josh 6:4, 15), Elijah's servant looking for rain 2,520 years (1 Ki 18:43), the child resurrected by Elisha sneezing 2,520 years (2 Ki 4:35), Naaman dipping in the river Jordan 2,520 years (2 Ki 5), and Nebuchadnezzar eating grass with the beasts of the field for 2,520 years (Dan 4).

The term "seven times" as used in Lev 26 refers to severity of punishment, and not to literal years. It was hoped that Israel's experience of more severe judgment and punishment in one period after another would bring the nation to repentance and reform. And, it was only after the 4th "seven times" experience that Israel was to be taken into captivity. It would be impossible to crowd 10,080 years into the nation's history or experience of the "times of the Gentiles" between the day of Moses to the captivities – one to Assyria in 749 B.C. and the other to Babylon 616 B.C. (2 Ki 17 and 25). See Chapter 3 for a brief study of the 8 great world empires in the times of the Gentiles.

In the "times of the Gentiles" which date from the Egyptian bondage in the days of Moses to our day, there have been already more than 3,700 years and there will be several more before the second advent of Christ when they will end (Rev 11:1-3; 12:6, 14; 13:5). Antichrist will be here at least 7 years before they can end (Dan 9:27) – and at the present writing he has not arrived on the scene yet.

The related term "the fullness of the Gentiles" means the same as "the times of the Gentiles," and not the cutting off of the Gentiles from salvation and the mercy of God at a certain time when God will turn to the Jews and save only them. There never has been a time when God would save only Jews and another time when He would save only Gentiles. His program has always been to save both Jews and Gentiles alike who would meet His conditions (Jn 3:16; Gal 3:8;

1 Tim 2:4-6; 2 Pet 3:9; Rev 22:17). He will save all Jews and Gentiles after the rapture and during the tribulation that will call upon Him (Acts 2:16-21; Rev 7:14; 22:17).

FALLACY 19: Jesus Christ did not offer rapture before the tribulation for anyone, in Lk 21:34-36.

TRUTH: In Lk 21:1-11 Christ gave some signs of His second advent — the same signs that we find in Mt 24:4-28. Then, in Lk 21:12-24 He mentioned some events that would happen to Jerusalem immediately in 70 A.D. saying that "before all these" signs of Lk 21:1-11 Jerusalem would be destroyed. He then (in Lk 21:25-33) came back to the subject of the signs of His second advent — those He had dealt with before in vss 1-11. And then, He told the disciples that there was a way of *escape from all these things* of Lk 21:1-11, 25-33; Mt 24:1-28.

Christ's conditions of ESCAPE FROM ALL THESE THINGS:

1. Take heed to yourselves (Lk 21:34).

2. Do not be overcharged with surfeiting, drunkenness, and cares of this life (Lk 21:34).

3. Do not let that day (when all these things shall happen) come upon you unawares (Lk 21:35).

4. Watch, and pray always, THAT YOU MAY BE ACCOUNTED WORTHY TO ESCAPE ALL THESE THINGS (of Lk 21:1-11, 25-33; Mt 24:1-28) that shall come to pass and to stand before the Son of Man (vs 36). If one wants to "escape all these things," then let him meet the conditions. If he will do this he can count on Christ to rapture him from the tribulation and literally fulfill His promise to all worthy ones. See proof 3, Chapter 10, below.

FALLACY 20: Dan 7:21 proves that Antichrist assails the church for a time, so it has to be here during his reign.

TRUTH: The church is not once mentioned in the book of Daniel, much less a war between the Church and Antichrist. Daniel is revealing, "what shall befall thy (Daniel's) people in the latter days" (Dan 9:24-27; 10:14; 11:40-45; 12:1-13). In no scripture do we find the church having an army with which to war against Antichrist or anyone else, but we do have scripture showing that Israel will fight against him (Dan 9:27; 11:40-45; 12:1-7; Zech 14:14; Mt 24:15-22; Rev 12:6, 14). Israel as a people is called "saints" (1 Sam 2:9; 2 Chr 6:41; Ps 16:3; 30:4; 31:23; 34:9; 85:8; 89:5-7; 97:10; 106:16; Dan 7:21, 25-27; Rev 11:18; 13:7; 18:24). The reference to "saints" in Dan 7:21 then, is not to the church which is raptured by the time of its fulfillment, but rather to Israel who will be involved in such warfare.

FALLACY 21: There is no time element mentioned in Scripture regarding the rapture.

TRUTH: There is no time element mentioned regarding any certain day or year, but there is of the church being raptured *before* "all these things" of Lk 21:1-11, 25-33; *before* the coming of the Antichrist; *before* the fulfillment of all of Rev 4:1-22:5; *before* the tribulation; and *before* the second advent takes place, for all raptured saints are in heaven eating a marriage supper with the Lamb (Rev 19:1-10) *before* the second advent begins (Rev 19:11-21). See Chapters 10-11.

FALLACY 22: The Gr. word *apantesis*, translated *meet* in 1 Th 4:17 means *returning with* and implies continuing in the same direction as at the starting point. It therefore refers to Christ meeting with the saints in the clouds and coming on down immediately to the earth. The word, which is used in three passages, does not mean to change direction at all, as proved by Paul in his continued journey to Rome after meeting saints from Rome as far as Three Tavers (Acts 28:15-16).

TRUTH: When Paul met saints at Three Taverns and continued to Rome, he did so because it was his original purpose in making this journey. He could have turned and continued in another direction after meeting these saints, if such a direction had been his purpose or desire. The Gr. word *apantesis* as well as the English word *meet* simply means "to meet" and it does not require one to continue in only one direction after that meeting. In the other passage where the word is used, besides 1 Th 4:17, it is the occasion of the 10 virgins meeting the bridegroom (Mt 25:1, 6), and there is nothing to indicate that the virgins continued from then on in the same direction that the bridegroom came from. There is no rule to govern the use of this word which limits its meaning to the continuance of persons who *meet* "in only one direction after they meet."

FALLACY 23: There is no rapture in the book of Revelation until the second advent in Rev 19:1-21.

TRUTH: Nothing is said in this particular scripture about a rapture, but much is said about the marriage supper of all saints in heaven (Rev 19:1-10) and the second advent which occurs afterward (Rev 19:11-21). The rapture precedes the tribulation and the marriage supper; the supper precedes the second advent; and the second advent precedes the Millennium (Rev 20:1-10). There will be several raptures before the second advent of Rev 19:11-21, as proved in Chapter 11, below. The rapture of the church and O. T. saints of Rev 5:8-10 will take place before the 7 seals, 7 trumpets, and 7 vials. Following this rapture will be that of the 144,000 Jews who will be raptured to heaven as the manchild of Rev 7:1-8; 9:4; 12:5; 14:1-5, all of this to happen before the second advent of Rev 19. And then, there will be the rapture of tribulation saints and the two witnesses who will be taken to heaven before the second advent (Rev 11:7-12; 15:1-4; 19:1-10). And so, there are several raptures reported in the book of Revelation and these take place before the second advent of Rev 19:11-21 which is simply the coming of Christ from heaven after the marriage supper with all the raptured saints, to reign on earth (Rev 19:11-21; Jude 14-15; Zech 14:1-9; Mt 24:29-31; 2 Th 1:7-10).

FALLACY 24: The fact that Jesus said that the resurrection would take place *in the last day* proves that the rapture of the church takes place at that time – the last day (Jn 6:39-54).

TRUTH: The Gr. word for *last* in this passage is *eschatos,* meaning furtherest, uttermost, remote, or end time. The end in this case does not refer to the last day of existence, for there will be no such day when time and days will come to an end forever. Day and night are eternal (Gen 8:22). The earth is eternal (Eccl 1:4; Ps 104:5). The term *last* day here refers to the end time of this age, and not to one particular day only. We know from Rev 20:4-15 that there will be 1,000 years between the time of the resurrection of the good and that of the bad, so there cannot be only one "last day" for all men to be resurrected. The term proves nothing as to when the rapture of the church will take place. That it will be before the tribulation is certain. See Chapters 10-11.

FALLACY 25: If we teach a rapture as a distinct coming of the Lord, and the second advent as another coming of the Lord 7 years later, then the rapture would be the second advent and the coming which followed would be a third advent.

TRUTH: That the rapture is a distinct coming of the Lord is clear, but it is not a coming down to the earth. It could never therefore, be the second advent to the earth, because at the time of the rapture the Lord comes only in the air or clouds surrounding the earth. The other coming of the Lord, to take place at least 7 years after the rapture, is the one and only second advent to the earth. Christ could come any number of times down to the clouds without continuing to the earth to set up His kingdom, just as a person might travel many times to Washington without ever going as far as New York.

FALLACY 26: There will be no such thing as one coming of Christ FOR His saints, and another coming WITH His saints.

TRUTH: The Bible teaches that Christ will come FOR His saints before the tribulation, and WITH His saints after the tribulation. Scriptures proving that Christ will come *for* His saints are: Jn 14:1-3; Lk 21:34-36; Eph 5:27; Phil 3:21; 1 Cor 15:23; Col 3:4; 1 Th 2:19-20; 3:13; 4:13-18; 5:1-11, 23; Jas 5:7-8; 2 Th 2:1. And, the purpose of coming *for* them as is required for the fulfillment of these passages, is to take them to heaven where they will enjoy their mansions and the marriage supper of the Lamb, as in Rev 19, before returning *with* Christ at the second advent to the earth. Scriptures teaching the coming of Christ *with* His saints are: Zech 14:5; Jude 14-15; 2 Th 1:7-10; Mt 16:27; 25:31; Rev 19:11-21.

FALLACY 27: The 144,000 Jews of Rev 7:1-8; 9:4; 12:5; 14:1-5 will never be raptured — they will go into the Millennium as natural earthly people.

TRUTH: The fact that the 144,000 Jews are sealed and protected to go through the trumpet judgments (Rev 7:1-8; 9:4); that they are raptured as the manchild (Rev 12:5; Isa 66:7-8; Dan 12:1), and that they are shown in heaven in Rev 14:1-5, having been redeemed FROM THE EARTH, and are without fault BEFORE THE THRONE, is proof that they will be raptured to heaven instead of going into the Millennium as earthly natural people. See Chapter 12.

FALLACY 28: The Holy Spirit ministry will cease on earth at the rapture of the church which follows the tribulation.

TRUTH: There is no such thing as the Holy Spirit ministry ceasing either before or after the rapture, before or after the tribulation, or before or after the Millennium. The Holy Spirit ministry will be eternal (Jn 14:16). It is to be during the tribulation (Acts 2:16-21; Zech 12:1-13:1) and the Millennium that the Holy Spirit will be poured out upon all flesh more than at any other time (Isa 32:15; 44:3; Joel 2:28-29). Regarding a rapture after the tribulation, this cannot be because all raptures will be over with by that time. Raptured saints will already be in heaven eating the marriage supper with Christ and remaining in readiness to return to earth with Him at the second advent which is the event that will take place after the tribulation, and not a rapture (Rev 19:1-21).

FALLACY 29: The church saints are the only people that will reign with Christ as kings and priests, and so to reign with Him the tribulation saints must be a part of the church which must remain here throughout the tribulation.

TRUTH: Tribulation saints will truly reign with Christ (Rev 20:4-6), but this does not prove they are a part of the church, nor does it prove that the church will be here during the tribulation. Church saints are not the only ones that will reign with Christ. All O. T. and N. T. saints will reign with Christ (Ps 149:6-8; 1 Cor 6; Rev 2:26-28; 5:8-10); the 144,000 will reign with Him (Rev 7:1-8; 9:4; 12:5, 14:1-5); and the tribulation saints and all who will have a part in the first resurrection will reign with Him (Rev 20:4-6). This means that all saints whether they are part of the N. T. church company or not will have their part in the reign of Christ.

FALLACY 30: Mt 24:14 proves that the church will be here during the tribulation because the gospel will be preached throughout this period.

TRUTH: Those who will preach the gospel during the tribulation period will not be a part of the church but people who have missed the rapture of the church, and will, in the tribulation period become saved and preach to others during that time. See Chapters 10-11.

FALLACY 31: The Gr. word for "taken" in Mt 24:37-42 is the same word translated "receive" in Jn 14:3 so both scriptures must refer to the same event — the rapture after the tribulation.

TRUTH: Mt 24:37-42 does not mention the rapture at all. Instead, the passage refers to the battle of Armageddon, as already proved in Chapter 6. Furthermore, the translation and use of any particular word in Scripture does not prove relationship of events or identify them as the same happenings. In the case of the Gr. word *paralambano* it is translated *take* many times (Mt 1:20; 2:13, 14, 20; 18:16); *took* (Mt 1:24; 2:14, 21; 20:17; 27:27); *taketh* (Mt 4:5, 8; 12:45; 17:1); *taken* (Mt 24:40-41); *received* (Mk 7:4; Jn 1:11; 1 Cor 11:23; 15:1, 3; Col 2:6); *receive* (Jn 14:3); and *receiving* (Heb 12:28). It is used of many subjects and, like so many of our English words, has different meanings. Its usage in Mt 24:37-42 referring to Armageddon cannot therefore limit its meaning to the same event, when used in another passage, as in the case of Jn 14:1-3 which refers to the rapture and not to the second advent which is at least 7 years later.

FALLACY 32: Mt 25:1-13 and Rev 19:1-10 refer to the same marriage of the Lamb on earth after the tribulation.

TRUTH: Contrary to the above, one casual reading of the two scriptures will reveal many points of contrast.

1. Mt 25:1-13 is a story of a marriage on earth, the marriage of a certain young man and young lady, which Jesus used to illustrate watchfulness in view of His second advent, while the marriage supper of Rev 19:1-10 is one that will be fulfilled literally as described — a supper to take place in heaven just before Christ and His saints start the second advent to the earth.

2. Mt 25:1-13 is an event on earth, while Rev 19:1-10 is an event in heaven.

3. Mt 25 was fulfilled when the young couple of the story became married, while Rev 19 is the prediction of a marriage supper of the Lamb which is yet to happen.

4. The marriage of Mt 25 took place nearly 2,000 years ago, while the marriage of Rev 19 is yet to take place, just before the second advent. The one is historical whereas the other is prophetical.

5. Not one person in the story of Mt 25 was resurrected from the dead in order to partake of the wedding supper, while all at the marriage supper of the Lamb in Rev 19 will be persons either resurrected from the dead or given immortality otherwise (1 Cor 15:51).

6. Not one at the wedding of Mt 25 was raptured, whereas all

attending the wedding supper of Rev 19 will have been raptured or they would not be in heaven at the supper.

FALLACY 33: Jesus never once mentioned a rapture as a separate and distinct coming from the second advent.

TRUTH: Jesus mentioned and made it very clear that before His coming to the earth to set up a kingdom He would come and take all saints to heaven to live with Him (Jn 14:1-3). And, He gave the assurance that every true saint of God would ESCAPE ALL THESE THINGS and STAND BEFORE THE SON OF MAN (Lk 21:34-36). Again, He made it clear that the church would be taken out of the world before the fulfillment of Rev 4:1-22:5, as will be proved in Chapter 10, below. Furthermore, He gave John a revelation of various companies of redeemed who would be raptured to heaven before the second advent (Rev 5:8-10; 12:5; 14:1-5; 15:1-5; 19:1-21).

FALLACY 34: The judgment seat of Christ and rewards to saints will be on earth after the second advent of Christ (Rev 19:11-21).

TRUTH: The judgment seat of Christ, the giving of rewards, and assigning the places of rulership in the coming kingdom will take place in heaven between the time of the rapture and the second advent. This is not the judgment of the nations at the second advent (see Chapter 6) which will be a judgment of living nations only, instead of the righteous who have been resurrected from the dead (Rev 11:18). By the time the saints land on earth with Christ at His second advent, they will already know their part in the battle of Armageddon as well as in the coming kingdom (1 Cor 3:11-15; 2 Cor 5:9-10; Rom 14:10). Not a statement in Scripture mentions a judgment of saints on earth or a distribution of their rewards at the second advent. Having already received their rewards and appointments to rulership at the judgment seat of Christ in heaven, they will, at the second advent take part with Him in the actual and literal establishment of the kingdom when "the kingdoms of this world are become the kingdoms of our Lord and of his Christ" (Rev 11:15). They will then take up their responsibilities in the kingdom, as kings and priests (Rev 5:10).

FALLACY 35: Since the great commission of Mt 28:19-20 was given to the church, and will be in force until the end of this age, it proves that the church will be on the earth all of this time.

TRUTH: The responsibility of the great commission is for all generations throughout this age, and also in the next one – the Millennium. Each generation that has come and gone has taken on the responsibility of evangelizing the world. And so it will be after the rapture of the church, even though it takes place at least 7 years before the end of this age. Those who are left, and become saved, will then carry on without the church, for they will have the same

Holy Spirit to enable them to continue the gospel program. It must be remembered that the gospel program was given first to Abraham (Gal 3:8) and to all Israel (Heb 2:1-4; 4:1-2). And, it will be carried on in the Millennium without the church of this age, for then it will be the Jewish responsibility again (Isa 2:1-4; 11:9; 52:15; Zech 8:23; 14:16-21). God has never left Himself without witness (Acts 14:17). In the tribulation period there will be the greatest revival of all, and that without the present generation of Christians of the church (Acts 2:16-21; Rev 7:14).

FALLACY 36: The only time "caught up" is used in the Bible is in 1 Th 4:16.

TRUTH: The Gr. word for "caught up" is "harpazo" and is used many times of persons and things being "caught up" or "snatched away by force" or "plucked up" or "taken by force." It is translated thus: of saints "caught up" to heaven (1 Th 4:17); of Paul being "caught up to the third heaven" (2 Cor 12:2, 4); of the manchild or 144,000 "caught up unto God and to his throne" (Rev 12:5); of the "catching" of sheep by wolves (Jn 10:12); to "pluck" men out of God's hands (Jn 10:28-29); of "pulling" men out of the fire (Jude 23); of the violent "taking" of the kingdom of heaven "by force" (Mt 11:12); of men coming "to take him (Jesus) by force" (Jn 6:15); of soldiers going down "to take him (Paul) by force" (Acts 23:10); of "catching away" the word out of the heart (Mt 13:19); and of Philip being "caught away" from one place to another (Acts 8:29).

The catching up of Paul and the manchild ended in heaven – a two way trip for Paul, and a one way trip for the 144,000 Jews as the manchild. The catching up of the saints in the raptures as in 1 Th 4:17 will also be a one way trip, for after that they are seen in heaven by John (Rev 5:8-10; 19:1-10).

FALLACY 37: Many people will survive the tribulation and be alive to be raptured at the second advent.

TRUTH: It is true that many people will survive the tribulation and be alive after it, and also after the second advent, but not one of them will be raptured and thereby changed bodily from mortality to immortality, as will be the case of saints raptured before the second advent. All raptures will be over with by that time and every person who will have part in the first resurrection will have already been raptured before the second advent. If we had no scripture but Rev 19 we would have enough proof that all raptured saints will be in heaven and will eat a marriage supper before the second advent begins. It is after this supper in heaven that Christ and His raptured saints will mount their horses and make the second advent to the earth.

Those who survive the tribulation must also survive the judgment of the nations of Mt 25:31-46; Dan 7:9-14, or they will be sent to hell. Those who do survive will simply enter the Millennium as earthly natural subjects of Christ and His raptured saints. This is proved in both Mt 13:39-43, 49-50 and Mt 25:30, 34, 41, 46.

It is clear from the above passages that, instead of being raptured, those who survive the tribulation and the following judgment will simply do as revealed in Mt 13:43 which says: "THEN shall the righteous shine forth as the sun in the kingdom of their Father." The same is referred to in Mt 25:34 which says: "THEN shall the King say unto them on his right hand, Come, ye blessed of my Father, inherit the kingdom prepared for you from the foundation of the world."

Chapter 10

7 Scriptural Proofs of the Rapture of the Church and O. T. saints before the future Tribulation

Proof 1: In 2 Th 2:1-12 we have a clear proof that the church and O. T. saints will be raptured *before* the day of the Lord, that is *before* the second advent, and *before* the revelation of the Antichrist, *before* Daniel's 70th week, *before* the future tribulation, and *before* the last 7 years of this age which ends with the second advent of Christ to the earth.

In 2 Th 2:1-4 Paul beseeches saints not to be deceived by any means or by anybody, as to the coming of the day of the Lord, or the second advent. The two things that were to precede the day of the Lord are:

1. "A great falling away" and
2. "That man of sin be revealed" (2 Th 2:3).

Besides these two things Paul revealed that a third great event would take place, this one to precede the day of the Lord or second advent, and also precede the revelation of the man of sin. He said, "he who now letteth (hindereth) will let (will hinder) UNTIL HE BE TAKEN OUT OF THE WAY. AND THEN shall that wicked be revealed" (2 Th 2:7-8). Thus it is clear that the hinderer of lawlessness will be taken out of the way before the Antichrist can come. "Our gathering together unto him" of 2 Th 2:1 and the hinderer of lawlessness "be taken out of the way" of 2 Th 2:7-8 refer to the same event — the rapture of the church and O. T. saints *before* the revelation of the Antichrist. AND THEN (when he who hinders lawlessness is taken out of the way) shall that wicked be revealed.

Two comings of the Lord from heaven, but only one coming to the earth

1. A coming of the Lord out of heaven FOR the saints *to meet them in the air* and to take them to heaven without coming to the earth (1 Th 1:10; 2:19-20; 3:13; 4:13-18; 5:1-11, 23; 2 Th 2:1, 7-8; Jn 14:1-3; Lk 21:34-36; Col 3:4; Eph 5:27; Jas 5:7-8; Rev 5:8-10; 19:1-10).

2. A coming of the Lord out of heaven WITH His previously raptured saints to bring them to the earth to fight at Armageddon and to set up a kingdom in the world for ever (Rev 19:1-21; Jude 14-15; 2 Th 1:7-10; 2:7-8; 1 Cor 15:24-28; Mt 16:27; 24:29-31; 25:31-46; Zech 14:1-5; Dan 2:44-45; 7:9-14; 18, 22, 27).

12 Truths of 2 Th 2:1-12 that the Thessalonians knew of:

1. That it was possible to be deceived about the rapture and the second advent (2 Th 1:1-3).

2. That the day of the Lord, or the second advent, was not at hand and therefore, it was not the time for the Lord to be here reigning on earth (2 Th 2:3).

3. That they were not to permit themselves to be deceived (2 Th 2:3).

4. That the day of the Lord would begin only at the second advent (2 Th 2:3; Zech 14:1-5).

5. That this day of the Lord, or the second advent, could not have already come because the great apostasy and the revelation of the man of sin had not yet come (2 Th 2:3).

6. That the man of sin will take over the Jewish temple at Jerusalem and declare himself to be God (2 Th 2:4). See Rev 13; 14:9-11; 15:1-4; 20:4-6; Dan 9:27; Mt 24:15-22, 29-31.

7. That the man of sin (the Wicked one or Antichrist) has a definite time to be revealed (2 Th 2:6-8).

8. That "he" who hinders lawlessness and holds back the man of sin will be entirely removed before he will fully come (2 Th 2:5-8).

9. That the mystery of lawlessness is already at work in the world (2 Th 2:7).

10. That Paul's doctrines had not changed regarding the rapture and the day of the Lord, as false teachers had reported, even forging a letter in his name (2 Th 2:2, 5).

11. That the man of sin (Antichrist) would be destroyed by Christ at the second advent when the day of the Lord begins (2 Th 2:7-8). See Dan 7:11; Rev 19:20; 20:10.

12. That Antichrist will come after the working of Satan with all power and great deceptions (2 Th 2:8-12. See Mt 24:24; Rev 13:1-18; Dan 8:24-25; 11:37-45).

7 other facts about the Rapture in 1 and 2 Thessalonians:

1. The church waits for Jesus to come from heaven (1 Th 1:10).

2. The church will be taken to glory (1 Th 2:12. See Col 3:4).

3. Soul winners will have great joy at this coming (1 Th 2:19-20).

4. The saints will be established unblameable *before God in heaven* (1 Th 3:13).

5. Both the dead and living in Christ will be raptured to heaven to live with Christ (1 Th 4:13-18. See Jn 14:1-3; Phil 3:21).

6. God has appointed all saved men to escape His latter day wrath on men (1 Th 5:1-11. See Lk 21:34-36).

7. Saints will be made whole in body, soul, and spirit at the rapture (1 Th 5:23. See Phil 3:21).

Who or What is the Hinderer of Lawlessness?

Paul definitely said that the hinderer of lawlessness would continue to hinder lawlessness UNTIL HE BE TAKEN OUT OF THE WAY. AND THEN shall that Wicked be revealed, whom the Lord shall destroy at His second advent (2 Th 2:7-8). If this question — who or what the hinderer of lawlessness is — can be settled the time of the rapture will be automatically settled.

3 things that hinder lawlessness in the world today:

1. Human governments (Gen 9:1-8; Rom 13; 1 Pet 2:14).
2. The Holy Spirit (Jn 14:16; 15:26; 16:7-11).
3. The church (Mt 5:13-16; 1 Cor 12:28; Rom 12:3-8; 1 Pet 4:10-19).

In no scripture in the two books to the Thessalonians did Paul mention governments or the Holy Spirit as being taken out of the world, but he repeatedly referred to the church as being raptured out of the world and from the earth (1 Th 1:10; 2:19-20; 3:13-18; 5:1-11, 23; 2 Th 2:1, 7-8). We must therefore conclude that the church is the hinderer of lawlessness, and for the following reasons.

1. *Human governments* will never be taken out of the world to permit the revelation of the Antichrist. He, himself, will even reign over 10 kingdoms when he comes (Rev 17:8-17). And, many other governments will be here in other parts of the earth throughout all the days that the man of sin (Antichrist) will be here (Dan 2:44-45; 7:9-14; Rev 16:13-16; Zech 14:1-5).

2. *The Holy Spirit* will never be taken from the world, for Jesus promised "that he may abide with you for ever" (Jn 14:16). In Acts 2:16-21; Zech 12:10-13:1, Mt 24:14; Rev 7:14; 19:10 and other scriptures we have much proof that the Holy Spirit will still be here throughout the tribulation and the reign of Antichrist. He therefore could not be the hinderer of lawlessness referred to, that will be taken out of the way.

3. *The church* will be taken out of the world by rapture, as stated in the above references. It is the only one of the above mentioned 3 hinderers of lawlessness that is to be taken out of the world, so it must be the hinderer of 2 Th 2:7-8.

That this hinderer of lawlessness will literally be taken out of the world is clear from the Gr. statement, "ek mesou genetai," which means, "out of the midst be gone (2 Th 2:7-8). The Gr. phrase "ek mesou" literally means "from among" and is so translated in the following scriptures: Mt 13:49; Acts 17:33; 23:10; 1 Cor 5:2; 2 Cor 6:17; Col 2:13-14; 2 Th 2:7. Whatever is referred to as the hinderer is being taken out of the way, and not being brought into the midst of men.

Out of 25 versions examined by this author, not one reads "born out of the midst of men" as said by some who teach that instead of referring to the revelation of Antichrist, this passage (2 Th 2:7-8) speaks of his birth. These versions render the passage in 13 different ways, and the thought in every one is not the birth of Antichrist but rather the fact that the hinderer of lawlessness is to be literally removed from the earth, from among men, before the revelation of that Wicked one.

The renderings of these versions are: "be removed" from the midst (4 times); "be gone" – not here (1 time); "be gotten out of the way" (3 times); "taken from the midst"—not born into the midst (1 time); "coming to be out of the midst" (1 time); "is taken out of the way" (2 times); "gone from the midst" (1 time); "the restraining power removed" (1 time); "disappear from the scene" (1 time); "be out of the way" (1 time); "steps out of the way" (1 time); "becomes out of the way" (1 time); "taken out of the way" (7 times).

Even if we believed that the Holy Spirit would be taken out of the world to permit the revelation of the man of sin, we could not possibly believe that He would abandon the church, leaving it, the body of Christ, in the world to go through terrible sufferings without Him. And so, the church would be taken out of the world with Him, and thus the rapture of the church before the tribulation, is proved either way.

Men have stumbled over the use of the pronoun "he" in 2 Th 2:7 for a long time and a great many teachers have not been able to bring themselves to the fact that a masculine pronoun could refer to the church when it has been universally taught that the church is the bride of Christ, a woman, a lady, and a virgin. If the pronoun "she" had been used in 2Th 2:7 every Bible scholar who teaches that the church is the bride of Christ would have automatically believed and taught that this "she" identified the church as the hinderer of lawlessness and would have used this as proof of the church being taken out of the world before the tribulation and revelation of the Antichrist.

The Church is not the Bride of Christ

That the church is not the bride of Christ is clear from many scriptures and facts about the church, and about the bride of Christ.

1. In no scripture is the church ever called the bride of Christ, though the fallacy can be found universally in commentaries, Bible textbooks, doctrine books, song books, and other Christian writings. Never once is this idea stated in the Bible, itself, though it does mention the bride of Christ and tells us exactly who it is. Read Rev 21:9-10 and see that the angel who said "I will shew thee the bride,

the Lamb's wife," shewed it to be "that great city, the holy Jerusalem, descending out of heaven from God." See also Rev 21:2 and 22:17. The inhabitants of the Heavenly Jerusalem are called "his wife" in Rev. 19:1-10. The idea is that all the redeemed of all ages who will go to live in that city will become a part of the Holy City, which is the bride, but to call any individual, or any company of saints, or any group of Christians "the bride" is unscriptural. They, as a whole, can be a part of the bride, but no single one of them and no one company of saints in any age can be said to be the bride of Christ. See Jn 14:1-3; Heb 11:11-16; 12:22-23; 13:14.

2. It is plain in Eph 2:14-15 and 4:13 that the church is a "man" and not a woman. Being the *body* of Christ who was a man and the head of the church, it is only to be expected that His body (the church) would be referred to as a man and not a woman. It cannot be that the head would be that of a man and the body that of a woman. And so, since the church is the body of Christ as stated in 1 Cor 12:13, 27; Eph 1:22-23; Col 1:18, 24, then the church is not to be considered a woman. Therefore, the masculine pronoun in 2 Th 2:7 is proper and the only one to use of the N. T. church. It is perfectly scriptural to use the pronoun "he" when referring to the whole body of Christ. The Bible uses it many times when referring to whole companies or nations of people made up of both men and women. For example, all the nation of Israel is called "he" (Dt 32:15; Isa 11:16; Josh 22:22).

3. Not once is the N. T. church called a woman, a lady, or a virgin. Furthermore, the church is never referred to by a feminine pronoun. Some think that Eph 5:22-31 would be an exception to this, but a closer reading of the passage will make the meaning clear. Paul illustrates the headship of Christ to the church and His relationship with it by comparing this headship and relationship to a similar headship and relationship which exist between a man and his wife. Christ and His church are one thing and the man and his wife are another, with the feminine pronoun referring to the woman who is the wife of the man — not to the church as the wife of Christ.

4. Some teachers use 2 Cor 11:1-2 to make the woman a symbol of the church, but Paul is not emphasizing the feminity of the church here. He is simply expressing his desire for his own converts to be pure like a virgin, so that they may be presented in all purity before God. The whole church is not referred to here at all.

5. Others use Gal 4:26 hoping to prove that the church is symbolized by a woman, but again, this is not the intention of the passage. The apostle expresses the idea that the Holy City is the headquarters and the source of all blessings, comparing the City to a mother as the source of blessings to her children. Using the woman of Rev 12 as a symbol of the church is missing the mark completely, for this woman is a symbol of Israel as a nation — and not the church

(Gen 37:9-10). Israel is clearly shown to be the wife of God in Isa 54:4-9; Hos 2:14-18.

Proof 2: Another proof of the rapture of the church and O. T. saints *before* the tribulation is found in Rev 1:19 and 4:1. All the dead and living in Christ at this point in time will be raptured to meet the Lord in the air to be taken to heaven to live in mansions, in the Father's house with Christ eternally (Jn 14:1-3; Lk 21:34-36; 1 Cor 15:23, 51-56; Eph 5:27; Col 3:4; 1 Th 2:19-20; 3:13; 4:13-18; 5:1-11, 23; Jas 5:7-8; Heb 11:10-16; 12:22-23; 13:14; Rev 5:8-10; 19:1-10).

Christ made it clear to John in Rev 1:19 and 4:1 that all the details of every prophecy in Rev 4:1-22:21 MUST BE AFTER THE CHURCHES. This is confirmed without controversy in the 3-fold division of the book of Revelation.

The Three Divisions of Revelation:

1. *"Write the things which thou hast seen,"* that is, write, as the first division of this book the vision that you saw of me (Christ) in the midst of the candlesticks in Rev 1:11-18 (Rev 1:19). This John did in the first chapter of the book.

2. *"Write the things which are,"* that is, write in the second division of the book of Revelation the things that I (Christ) will tell you to write about concerning the churches, or concerning the church on earth. This John did in Rev 2:1-3:22 (Rev 1:19).

3. *"Write the things which must be hereafter,"* that is, write as the third and last division of the book of Revelation things that I (Christ) will show you after you have completed things concerning the churches. These last things do not concern the things of the churches — they concern events after the church age. These things to happen after the church age were recorded by John in Rev 4:1-22:21 (Rev 1:19).

The Key to the Book of Revelation

If one will accept this simple 3-fold division of Revelation, as in the above, and keep every detail of the events in the proper division as revealed, this will truly serve as the KEY to an understanding of the entire book. All that is required for an understanding of these events is to take them literally as things to happen on the earth from John's day forward into all eternity to come, making sure above all else, that each event is put in its proper place or order of events as they are revealed — each in its own division, not mixing those things concerning the church with those things which must be after the churches.

We have in the things concerning the churches, and the events which must be after the churches two separate and distinct series of happenings that cover two separate and distinct periods of time — one period covering the church age (Rev 2:1-3:22), and the other covering the time from the end of the church period, or church age, into all eternity to come (Rev 4:1-22:5). Whenever we see that "the things which are" belong to the church age, and that "the things which *must be* after the things which are" belong to the period from the close of the church age on into all eternity, then the entire book becomes as simple to understand as Jn 3:16. The main thing to keep in mind is that Rev 4:1-22:21 will be fulfilled AFTER the church age, and therefore, after the rapture of the church. Not one of these latter day details has anything to do with the church age.

Summary of things after the Rapture — after the Church Age:

1. Events in heaven that John saw after he arrived there, as in Rev 4:1, including the raptured church and O. T. saints who were seen in heaven by this time, being a fulfillment of things revealed here, for the first time, as happening AFTER THE CHURCHES (Rev. 4:1-5:14). The raptured church saints are definitely pictured as being in heaven at this point (Rev 5:8-10).

2. Events of Daniel's 70th week, or the last 7 years of this age between the events which John saw in heaven in Rev 4 and 5 and the second advent in Rev 19:11-21. This period covers all the 7 seals, 7 trumpets, and 7 vials, and all other details regarding the two witnesses (Rev 11:3-12), the woman and the manchild (Rev 12), the two beasts (Rev 13:1-14:20); and the great whore (Rev 17).

3. The marriage supper of the Lamb and the second advent (Rev 19:1-21).

4. The Millennium — 1,000-year reign of Christ to put down all rebellion on earth (Rev 10:1-6; 1 Cor 15:24-28; Eph 1:10).

5. Events ending the 1,000-year reign of Christ including the renovation of the heavens and the earth by fire (Rev 20:7-15; 2 Pet 3:10-13; Heb 1:10-12; 12:26-29).

6. Events of the eternal new heaven and the new earth (Rev 21-22; Isa 65:17; 66:22-24; 2 Pet 3:10-13).

From the above we can see that it would be erroneous to make various details of history a part of things yet to happen which are the 7 seals, 7 trumpets, 7 vials, and other events including the woman and the manchild of Rev 12. It would be erroneous to say for instance, that the ascension of Christ 65 years before John wrote the book of Revelation, was actually the ascension of the manchild (Rev 12:5) in the middle of events WHICH MUST BE AFTER THE CHURCHES. In comparing 25 versions with the King James Version, the author has found that every one is in agreement with the fact that the prophecies of Rev 4:1 on through the 22nd chapter of the book are to be fulfilled in detail AFTER THE CHURCHES, that is, after the church age — and this is in agreement with the 3-fold division of Revelation, as stated above.

To quote various renderings of Rev 4:1 one says, "Come up here, and I will show you what must take place hereafter," another says "what must come to pass after this," and others say "which are to happen in the future" and "what things must come to pass," all referring to what should happen after the churches which John had just completed writing about in the second division of his book (Rev 2:1-3:22).

Proof 3: Another proof of a rapture of the church and O. T. saints *before* the tribulation lies in the literal fulfillment of Lk 21:34-36. Christ personally promised all true believers who would meet the conditions that they would "ESCAPE ALL THESE THINGS" and "STAND BEFORE THE SON OF MAN." The things that the "worthy" ones were to escape are those listed in Lk 21:1-11, 25-33; Mt 24:1-25:46; Mk 13 and Rev 4:1-18:24. The only way they could do this would be to be raptured before these events took place. To escape means that they would not suffer or have to endure these things; and to stand before the Son of man means that they would be raptured bodily so as to be able to stand before Him in bodily presence. They will therefore literally rise "to meet him in the air" and be received by Christ to go up to heaven to live with Him (Jn 14:1-3; 1 Cor 15:23, 51-54; Eph 5:27; Phil 3:21; Col 3:4; 1 Th 2:19-20; 3:13; 4:13-18; 5:1-11, 23; 2 Th 2:1, 7-8; Jas 5:7-8; 1 Jn 2:28; 3:1-3; Rev 1:19; 4:1; 5:8-10; 19:1-10).

The Gr. word for *escape* in Lk 21:36 is *ekpheugo,* meaning to flee out of the way (Acts 19:16); to get away (Acts 16:27); and to escape danger and even hell (Lk 21:36; Rom 2:3; 2 Cor 11:33; 1 Th 5:1-4; Heb 2:3; 12:25).

Proof 4: A proof of a rapture of the church and O. T. saints *before* the tribulation is found in Rev 5:8-10. Here we have the raptured saints of all past ages up to this point already in heaven having been already redeemed and raptured to heaven. They are the "kings and priests" from "every kindred, and tongue, and people, and nation" who will reign on the earth. They are in heaven at this point in the fulfillment of Rev 4:1-22:21, all of which *must be fulfilled after the churches.* The fact that they are here revealed as already having been redeemed and raptured cannot be denied. They are pre-tribulation saints and they are in heaven at the very beginning of the tribulation which starts in the first seal and continues throughout the entire 7 seals, the 7 trumpets, and the 7 vials of Rev 6:1-16:21; 18:1-24. The tribulation saints are those that are martyred in this 70th week of Daniel (Rev 6:9-11; 7:9-17; 14:9-13;

15:1-5; 20:4-7; Dan 7:21; 9:27). There is a special song of redemption related to the pre-tribulation saints (Rev 5:8-10) that is entirely different from the song sung 3½ years later by the 144,000 (Rev 14:1-5), and the one sung 7 years later by the tribulation saints (Rev 15:1-5).

Proof 5: In 1 Th 5:1-11 Paul makes it plain that the **wrath** of God that begins in the 6th seal of Rev 6:12-17 in the first 3½ years of Daniel's 70th week is not "appointed" for the church, but for the ungodly world. He said, "God hath not appointed us to wrath, but to obtain salvation (deliverance) by our Lord Jesus Christ" so that both the dead and the living in Christ can live together in the rapture (1 Th 5:9-11). In view of this deliverance for both the dead, and the living in Christ at the rapture, we are to be comforted (1 Th 4:18; 5:11). And, since this wrath begins in the first part or in the first 3½ years of Daniel's 70th week, at the point of the 6th seal, then the church will be raptured before that. And furthermore, since the raptured saints are seen in heaven − in Rev 5:8-10 − BEFORE the first seal begins we must then conclude that the rapture takes place before any of the seals begin.

Proof 6: The enthroned elders of Rev 4:4, 10; 5:5-8, 11, 14; 7:11, 13; 11:16; 14:3; and 19:4 being seated on 24 thrones around the throne of God as representatives of the raptured saints of Rev 5:8-10 is proof that they are not only redeemed, but that they are also raptured by this time, that is, before the 7 seals, 7 trumpets and 7 vials begin. The fact that they are seen in heaven in Rev 5 at a time before the rapture of the 144,000 (Rev 14:1-5) and before the rapture of the tribulation saints (Rev 15:1-4) makes it clear that the enthroned elders are representatives of the church and O. T. saints, and not representatives of these other groups raptured later.

Proof 7: The fact that Rev 1:1-3:22 deals only with the church on earth, and Rev 4-19 deals with Israel gives us another proof of a rapture of the church and O. T. saints *before* the tribulation. Every individual is identified and recognized by his own features and characteristics. Even so in this case, a body of individuals is identified by its many features, characteristics, and peculiarities. If the church is seen on earth and is being dealt with by God during the tribulation in chapters 4-19 in the book of Revelation then we must see its earmarks. But they are not to be found there. The terms "church" and "churches" are not found once in this part of the book of Revelation. On the other hand, there are evidences of Israel everywhere in this section. And this fact is most striking: Israel is not mentioned at all in Rev 1:1-3:22 which deals only with the church on earth. This fact shows that the two different institutions are dealt with in different parts of the book of Revelation − first, the church until its rapture in Rev 1:1-3:22, and then, Israel after the rapture of the church, in Rev 4:1-22:5, beginning with Rev 4:1.

The Hebrew Character of Revelation after Rev 1-3:

1. The word "Lamb" is used of Christ 27 times after Rev 1-3 (which deals with the church age) and not once in these first three chapters of the book. It is never used by Paul in his epistles to the churches; and outside the book of Revelation it is used only in Jn 1:29, 36; Acts 8:32; 1 Pet 1:19. The Lamb is the antitype of all Jewish sacrifices.

2. "The Lion of the tribe of Juda" and "the Root of David" (Rev 5:5) show a Jewish connection.

3. The 144,000 of Rev 7:1-8; 9:4; 12:5; 14:1-5 are Jewish as well as the woman and her remnant.

4. The events of the seals, trumpets, and vials are a partial repetition of the plagues in Egypt which took place at a time when the Gentiles were seeking to destroy Israel (Rev 6:1-19:21).

5. The tribulation of Rev 6:1-19:21 concerns Israel in particular (see Chapter 2).

6. Daniel's 70th week will be fulfilled in Rev 6:1-19:21 which definitely concerns "thy people" (Israel) and "thy city" (Jerusalem) as indicated in Dan 9:24-27. The middle and last 3½ years of this Week are mentioned many times in connection with Israel but not in connection with the church (Dan 7:21, 25; 9:27; 12:1-7; Mt 24:15-22; Rev 11:1-12; 12:5, 14; 13:5).

7. The ministry of the angel around the altar (Rev 8:2-5) and the horns of the altar (Rev 9:13; 11:1; 14:19; 16:7) are familiar only to Israel.

8. The temple and its worship, the altar, the court of the Gentiles, the Holy City, olive trees, the candlesticks (Rev 11:4), the ark of the covenant (Rev 11:1-19; Zech 4:14; Mal 4:5-6) and other details here are Jewish — not details related to church worship.

9. "The kingdoms of this world" becoming those of God and of Christ is strictly Jewish in prediction and in fulfillment, being mentioned hundreds of times in the Jewish O. T. as well as in the N. T. (Lk 1:32-33; Acts 1:6-7; Rev 11:15, etc.).

10. The dragon, the beast, and the false prophet (Rev 13:1-19:21) are referred to many times in Jewish prophecies in O. T. books whereas the church is not once mentioned as being here when these prophecies are being fulfilled.

11. Michael (Rev 12:7-12) is truly Jewish as he is the prince of Israel (Dan 10:13-31; 12:1-9). He is never mentioned in connection with the church.

12. Literal Babylon of Rev 14:8; 16:17-21; 18:1-24 is solely a Jewish reference and the predictions will be fulfilled when many other Jewish predictions are fulfilled (Isa 13-14; Zech 5; Jer 50-51). Babylon was the place where Israel was held captive for many years (Jer 25).

13. Armageddon of Rev 19 is Jewish (Zech 14:1-14).

Chapter 11

4 Future exclusive Raptures before the Second Advent:

There will be no rapture, no ressurection of any man, and no person "in Christ" raptured at the second advent. No one, dead or alive, will be raptured at this point. By this time when Christ leaves heaven through the open door of Rev 19:11 all raptures will have taken place and the first resurrection will be completed. Though there will be multitudes of living human beings on the earth who will be classed as "the good," "the righteous," "the just," "the holy," "the elect," and "brethren" of Christ — people who have been born again — not one of them will be raptured at His second advent. The marriage supper will have taken place before the second advent and every person having a part in the first resurrection will have been raptured and will have shared in the supper just before the second advent begins. Those "in Christ" on earth at this point will simply go into the eternal earthly kingdom as natural people to be subjects of Christ and the raptured saints who will become rulers of the kingdom (1 Cor 6; Rev 1:5; 5:10; 20:4-6; 22:4-5).

There will be FOUR EXCLUSIVE RAPTURES OF FOUR EXCLUSIVE COMPANIES OF SAINTS BETWEEN NOW AND THE SECOND COMING OF CHRIST, as follows:

(1) The first future exclusive Rapture

This will be that of the church and the O. T. saints of Rev 5:8-10. Among the first 12 scenes John saw in heaven—scenes that, as he was told, MUST BE AFTER THE CHURCHES (Rev 4:1-22:5) one was the first company of exclusive saints to be raptured to heaven. John was told to "Come up hither, and I will show thee things which must be hereafter" (Rev 4:1), and immediately he was raptured from the Isle of Patmos to heaven where he saw the first things WHICH MUST BE AFTER THE CHURCHES. He saw God, the Lamb, the 7 lamps of fire, the 24 elders, the 4 living creatures, the sea of glass, the book with 7 seals, the various companies of creatures in worship to God and the Lamb, and finally the first raptured saints in heaven — all of these being events which must be after the churches. These saints are referred to as being redeemed by the blood of the Lamb from "every kindred, and tongue, and people, and nation" and as being already made "kings" and "priests" to God to reign on the earth (Rev 5:8-10).

Every scene in these two chapters of Revelation 4 and 5 pictures these saints as being already raptured and present in heaven when the

Lamb took the 7-sealed book out of the hand of God so as to break the seals. They were in heaven to witness every time one of the seals was broken and the contents revealed, and they continued in heaven while every one of the 7 trumpets, and the 7 vials, and all the other events of Rev 4:1-19:10 were being fulfilled before the second advent of Rev 19:11-21, at which time the marriage supper would be over and the second advent begun.

(2) The second future exclusive Rapture

The 144,000 Jews are the second exclusive company of saints to be raptured from the earth to go to heaven to live until the second advent begins which will be after the marriage supper pictured in Rev 19:1-21. This will be a rapture 3½ years *after* the church and O. T. saints are raptured (Rev 5:8-10) and 3½ years *before* the second advent (Rev 19:11-21). In Rev 7:1-8 we see that the 144,000 are sealed to be protected from the plagues of the 7 trumpet judgments. It was said to the first four trumpet judgment angels "Hurt not the earth, neither the sea, nor the trees, till we have sealed the servants of our God in their foreheads" (Rev 7:3). And, the 5th and 6th trumpet judgment angels were told to hurt only those men which have not the seal of God (God's name) in their foreheads (Rev 9:4; 14:1-5). The 144,000 will be raptured to "God and to his throne" as the manchild of Rev 12:5, and they are next seen in heaven singing an exclusive song that no man can sing but them—the 144,000 Jews of all these scriptures.

The 144,000 Jews of Rev 7:1-8; 9:4; 12:5; 14:1-5 are referred to in other prophecies concerning Israel and the manchild. In fact, Isa 66:7-8 speaks of the nation of Israel bringing forth the **manchild** at the time of her great travail or tribulation, saying: "Before she travailed, she brought forth; before her pain came, she was delivered of a manchild . . . for as soon as Zion travailed, she brought forth her children." Vs 8 of this scripture refers to Israel being born again as a nation, and vs 7 says "before" this travail of Israel to bring forth she brought forth a manchild. That is, **before** she travails for her own birth in the Spirit as a nation, she will be delivered of a manchild. That Israel will be born again by the Spirit at the second advent of Christ is plainly revealed in Zech 12:10-13:1; Rom 11:25-29.

Daniel also predicted that every one born again in Israel at the time "Michael stands up" to cast Satan and his angels out of heaven, every Jew who has his name in the book of life will be raptured or delivered (Dan 12:1; Rev 7:1-8; 12:7-12). Rev 7:1-8 and 14:1-5 tell us how many will have their names in the book of life at the time the manchild is raptured — 144,000 of them. Both Daniel (Dan 12:1-7) and Revelation (Rev 12:1-17) speak of the manchild, the 144,000

Jews, as being raptured 1,260 days before the second advent begins after the marriage supper.

This travail or great tribulation of Israel is referred to by Moses (Dt 4:30); Jeremiah (Jer 30:6-7); Daniel (Dan 12:1); Jesus (Mt 24:15-22); and John (Rev 7:14), but not once is it referred to as happening to the church or Christians of this present age. The "great" tribulation of Jezebel's followers, and the 10 days of tribulation of the church at Smyrna (Rev 2:10, 22) were local tribulations and are now already in the past, but the "great tribulation" yet to come, as referred to in the above scriptures, will be fulfilled only in Daniel's 70th week, as explained in Chapter 2, above. We must therefore conclude that the 144,000 will be raptured as an exclusive company of saints, and not as a part of the church or any other company of raptured saints.

(3) The third future exclusive Rapture

The tribulation saints will make up the third distinct company who will be saved and raptured out of the tribulation period as a group separate from the church (Rev 6:9-11; 7:9-17; 13:7; 14:12-13; 15:1-4; 17:7; 20:1-4). All these martyrs are to be saved AFTER the church and O. T. saints have been raptured and are in heaven (Rev 5:8-10). The first ones of this tribulation company of saints were told to wait until all who were to be martyred in the tribulation would be killed, and then their death would be avenged (Rev 6:9-11). These, without exception, are martyrs of the future tribulation, and not one will be martyred during the church age. All the scriptures about them are found in Rev 4:1-19:10, which must be fulfilled AFTER THE CHURCHES (See Proof 2, chapter 10). Most of these martyrs will be slain by the Antichrist (Rev 7:14; 13:7; 14:12-13; 15:1-5; 20:1-4). The lesser part will be killed by the great whore of Rev 17:6-7.

That they will all be raptured as a separate and distinct company of martyrs of the tribulation period is clear from the fact that they are seen in heaven singing their own redemptive song, by themselves and toward the latter part of the tribulation (Rev 15:1-4). These mainly will be the ones that will get "the victory over the beast (who reigns only the last 3½ years of this age, Rev 13:5), and over his image, and over his mark, and over the number of his name" (Rev 15:1-4). They are spoken of as being beheaded for Christ by the beast (Rev 20:4-6).

(4) The fourth future exclusive Rapture

The two witnesses of Rev 11:2-12 will be the fourth and last of the exclusive raptures of the future. They will be partakers of a rapture all by themselves after they are martyred at the end of their

3½ year ministry on earth. A great voice from heaven will say, "Come up hither," and they will then *ascend up to heaven* (Rev 11:7-12). See other scriptures about their ministry in Mal 4:5-6; Zech 4:14; Ezek 20:33-44.

All these separate raptures take place at different points in time — BEFORE and DURING Daniel's 70th week, ending with the rapture of the two witnesses, and BEFORE the second advent of Christ to the earth with all the raptured saints and angels. We cannot therefore teach that there will be no rapture at all until at the time of the second advent, for the above four mentioned future exclusive raptures prove otherwise.

Chapter 12

The Sun-clothed Woman and Manchild

It is imperative that we have a clear understanding of the sun-clothed woman and the manchild and their relationship to many last day events, especially the various raptures and the second coming of Jesus Christ. Note the following facts and scriptures in the Bible.

The Sun-clothed Woman is Jewish

1. Jacob interpreted the same symbolism as referring to the nation of Israel (Gen 37:9-11).

2. Israel is referred to as a woman, the wife of God in Isa 54:1-6; Jer 3; Hos 2:14-18.

3. The travail of the woman in Rev 12 is the same thing as the travail of Israel in Isa 66:7-8; Mic 5:3-10; Jer 4:31; 6:24; 13:21; 30:7; Mt 24:8, 15-22; Dan 12:1.

4. The persecution and flight of the woman of Rev 12 refers to the defeat and flight of Israel in the middle of Daniel's 70th week, as predicted in Isa 16:1-5; Ps 60; Ezek 20:33-44; Dan 9:27; 11:40-45; Jer 30:6-7; Hos 2:14-18; Mt 24:15-22.

The Manchild is Jewish — The Manchild is the 144,000 Jews

1. Since the sun-clothed woman of Rev 12 is Jewish, as proved above, then the manchild that she produces must also be Jewish. This is verified by the fact that God's unfailing law is that everything produces "after his own kind" (Gen 1:11-12, 21-25; 6:20; 7:14; Lev 11:14-29; Dt 14:13-18; Jas 3:7). A Jewish mother then produces a Jewish child, and such is the case of the woman of Rev 12 and her child.

2. The manchild being Jewish, we must find some Jews to fit the requirements—some we can identify in Rev 4:1-22:21, in the events that both God and Christ said MUST BE AFTER THE CHURCHES of Rev 1-3. There is only one group of Jews in these chapters of Revelation 4-22 that could possibly be the manchild, and that is the 144,000 of Rev 7:1-8; 9:4; 12:5; 14:1-5. In Rev 7:3 and 14:1 they are seen sealed with the Father's name in their foreheads. The seal then is not as some teach, the keeping of Saturday as the sabbath. It is literally the Father's name written on the forehead. See also Rev 3:12. It was said to the first 4 trumpet judgment angels to "Hurt not the earth, neither the sea, nor the trees, till we have sealed the servants of our God in their foreheads" (Rev 7:2-3). Special direction was given to the 5th and 6th trumpet judgment angels not to hurt the 144,000 Jews (Rev 9:4).

In Rev 12:5 they are seen "caught up to God and to his throne" as the manchild. Next, we find the 144,000 in heaven (in Rev 14:1-5), and we are also shown what they are doing when they reach heaven. They are singing a song that no man can sing but the 144,000 "which were redeemed (and raptured) FROM (away from) the earth" and we see that "they are without fault BEFORE THE THRONE OF GOD."

3. Some teach that the woman is the virgin Mary and not Israel as a nation, while others teach that she is the church, or Christendom. And some teach that the birth of the manchild is a record of the historical birth of Christ by Mary, and the manchild being caught up to God is a reference to the historical ascension of Christ to heaven — events that had happened some 65 years before John wrote the book of Revelation. But, as shown in Proof 2 of Chapter 10 in the study of "The Three Divisions of Revelation," the birth of and the catching away of the manchild (in Rev 12) are events that are to occur in the very middle of the things WHICH MUST BE AFTER THE CHURCHES. Therefore, it would be erroneous to bring such historical facts into the prophecies that are yet to be fulfilled — and there is no need to do this when we have clear evidence of a Jewish manchild being produced by a Jewish mother at the time designated for these events, in the future.

One of the reasons often given for teaching that Christ is the manchild of Rev 12 is the fact that the manchild will rule the nations with a rod of iron (Rev 12:5), and the same is predicted of Christ in Ps 2:9. But, it must be remembered that not only Christ and the manchild but also all the redeemed and raptured saints of all ages, those who have a part in the first resurrection, will also "live and reign with Christ" with a rod of iron. Rev 2:26-27 states clearly that "he that overcometh, and keepth my works unto the end, to him will I give power over the nations; And he shall rule them with a rod of iron." See also Ps 149:6-9; Dan 7:18, 22, 27; 1 Cor 6; Rev 5:10; 20:4-6. It remains then that the manchild being only one among many who will rule with a rod of iron, he can and will fulfill Rev. 12:5.

4. The manchild symbolizes a living company of Jews — not a company wherein some of them are dead and awaiting a resurrection as in the case of the rapture of the church. They are all alive and will be raptured alive as the manchild of Rev 12:5; Isa 66:7-8; Dan 12:1. No woman could bring forth a part-dead and part-living child. In Rev 12:1-4 we see the dragon standing before the woman hoping to devour her child as soon as it is born, but he is defeated in his purpose because the manchild is raptured immediately at birth. Then the woman, the main part of the nation of Israel left after this rapture of the manchild or 144,000, will flee into the wilderness (Rev 12:6, 14; Isa 16:1-5; Ezek 20:33-44; Hos 2:14-18; Mt 24:15-22).

5. An examination of Rev 7 and 14 shows the 144,000 of Israel to be the same company of people who are symbolized by the manchild. The sealing of both companies in the forehead (Rev 7:1-3; 14:1), the uniqueness of their number (Rev 7:4; 14:1), and their history prove this. In Rev 7 and 14 we also have their origin, destiny, time of rapture, place and position in heaven, and their occupation around the throne of God (Rev 7:1-8; 9:4; 12:5; 14:1-5).

6. The time of the rapture of the manchild proves that the reference is to the 144,000 who are caught up to God and to His throne. They are to be raptured in order to be in heaven in fulfillment of Rev 14:1-5 after remaining on earth to fulfill every scripture about them which requires fulfillment before the catching up of the manchild (Rev 7:1-8; 9:4; 12:5). This rapture is at the time of the 7th trumpet and the casting of Satan out of heaven (Rev 11:15; 12:7-12), and 1,260 days before the second advent (Rev 12:5-6, 14; 13:5). Recognizing the manchild and the 144,000 to be the same company of people, results in all problems being solved regarding the subject. Otherwise, the history of the manchild is not complete, and various questions remain. How and when are the 144,000 to be raptured? And, where is the account of their rapture?

7. The place where the 144,000 are seen to be — the heavenly mount Sion — proves that they were translated as the manchild to heaven (Rev 14:1-5; Heb 11:10-16; 12:22-23; 13:14; Jn 14:1-3).

8. The protection of the 144,000 on earth (Rev 7:1-8; 9:4), and their privileges and blessings shown to occur in heaven after the catching up of the manchild, prove that all these events take place with the same people, and at the same time (Rev 14:1-5). And, all of this shows them to be a separate and distinct company from all other groups of redeemed.

9. The 144,000 are to be "firstfruits" unto God and the Lamb (Rev 14:4), and this requires them to be saved and raptured after the "firstfruits" of Israel in the N. T. church who were saved about 2,000 years before. The 144,000 are to be the first Jews saved after the church is completed and after its rapture which takes place before the events of Rev 4:1-19:21 begin to be fulfilled — events WHICH MUST BE AFTER THE CHURCHES.

The 144,000 cannot be the Woman or the Remnant because:

1. The woman symbolizes the whole nation of Israel in Judea in the last days, whereas the manchild or 144,000 symbolizes a smaller part of the nation of Israel, and the remnant of the woman refers to a few who will be left in Judea. When Antichrist breaks his covenant with Israel and defeats them in battle, the woman or main body of Israel in Judea will flee into the mountains (Mt 24:15-22; Rev 12:6, 14), the 144,000 or every saved person in Israel at that time, will be

raptured (Isa 66:7-8; Dan 12:1; Rev 12:5), and the remnant of Israel will remain in their own land, not fleeing from the Antichrist (Rev 12:17).

2. The woman and the remnant will remain earthly people, while the 144,000 will become heavenly (Rev 12:1-17; 14:1-5).

3. The woman and the remnant will be in travail, while the 144,000 will not be (Isa 66:7-8; Dan 12:1; Rev 12:1-17).

4. The woman will bring forth a manchild, the 144,000, but neither the remnant nor the 144,000 are to bring forth such a child (Rev 12:1-5; Isa 66:7-8).

5. A company will be taken from the woman to heaven (the 144,000) whereas the woman, herself, and the remnant will be left on earth (Rev 12:6, 13-17). They cannot and will not be caught up to God and to His throne as the 144,000 will be (Rev 12:5; 14:1-5).

6. Neither the number of those in the company symbolized by the woman, nor the number of those in the remnant is given but the number of the manchild, the 144,000, is (Rev 7:1-8; 14:1-5).

7. Neither the woman nor the remnant are sealed for protection, while the 144,000 will be (Rev 7:1-8; 14:1-5). Neither the woman nor the remnant will be protected from the plagues of the trumpets, but the manchild or the 144,000 will be (Rev 7:1-8; 9:4; 12:5).

8. The 144,000 are not seen or mentioned as being on earth after the rapture of the manchild, but the woman and remnant are (Rev 12:1-4, 6-17).

9. The manchild or the 144,000 escape the dragon by rapture (Rev 12:5), while the woman and her remnant will escape by the earth swallowing up one of Satan's armies (Rev 12:13-17), and by God causing Antichrist to turn his efforts away from them until later (Dan 11:44; Mt 24:22).

10. The manchild or the 144,000 will have their names written in the book of life and will be ready for rapture out of the great tribulation, while the woman and remnant are not to be saved until later (Isa 66:7-8; Dan 12:1; Rev 7:1-8; 9:4; 12:5; 14:1-5).

Chapter 13

20 Contrasts between the Rapture and the Second Advent

1. The rapture is a *going up to heaven* of all saved men of all past ages (Jn 14:1-3; Col 3:4; Jas 5:7-8; Rev 5:8-10; 19:1-10), whereas the second advent is a *coming down from heaven to earth* of the same people (Rev 19:11-21; Jude 14-15; 2 Th 1:7-10; Mt 16:27; 24:29-31; 25:31-46; Zech 14:1-9).

2. The rapture is a coming of Christ from heaven to the clouds (not to the earth) FOR the saints, both dead (who will be resurrected) and alive to take them to heaven (1 Th 4:16), while the second advent is a coming from heaven WITH the previously raptured saints to set up a kingdom and rule eternally (Zech 14:1-9; Jude 14-15; Rev 11:15; 19:11-21; 22:4-5; 2 Th 1:7-10; Mt 25:31-46; Isa 9:6-7; Dan 2:44-45; 7:9-15, 18, 22, 27; Lk 1:32-36).

3. Our goal in the rapture is heaven to live with Christ in our mansions (Jn 14:1-3; 1 Th 2:19-26; 3:13; 4:13-18; 5:1-11, 23; Rev 5:8-10; 19:1-10; Col 3:4; Jas 5:7-8); while the goal in the second advent is to leave heaven for the earth to reign forever (Zech 14; Jude 14-15; Rev 11:15; 19:11-20:10).

4. At the rapture Christ does not come to destroy the Antichrist or any other wicked man but to remove the hinderer of lawlessness (the church, Chapter 10, Proof 1), so that the Antichrist can come (2 Th 2:17-8), while at the second advent Christ comes back to the earth with all saints of all ages to destroy Antichrist and multitudes of wicked men (2 Th 2:7-8; Dan 7:11; Jude 14-15; Rev 19:11-21. See also Mt 24:37-42; 25:31-46; Ezek 38-39; Zech 14).

5. At the rapture Christ comes from heaven to the clouds only (not to the earth) to take the good from among the bad (Jn 5:28-29; Jn 14:1-3; Lk 21:34-36; 1 Cor 15:23, 51-54; Phil 3:21; Col 3:4; 1 Th 4:16-18; Jas 5:7-8), while at the second advent, years later, He comes to the earth with His raptured saints to take the bad from among the good (Mt 13:30, 39-43, 49-50; 24:29-31, 37-42; Jude 14-15; Ezek 38-39; Zech 14; Rev 19:11-21).

6. At the rapture only those qualified for heaven will be raptured (Jn 14:1-3; Lk 21:34-36; 1 Cor 15:23; 1 Th 4:16; Rev 20:4-6), only those who are born again will be changed from mortality to immortality and go to heaven whereas, at the second advent any and all men qualified to live on the earth as citizens will be permitted to continue as natural people into the next age; without any change from mortality to immortality (Mt 25:31-46; Zech 8:23; 14:1-21; Isa 2:2-4; 66:19-21; Dan 2:44-45; 7:9-14; 1 Cor 15:24-28; Rev 2:27-28; 11:15; 20:4-6).

7. At the rapture there will be no battle of Armageddon (Jn 14:1-3; Lk 21:34-36; 1 Cor 15:23, 51–54; 1 Th 4:16), while at the second advent Armageddon will be fought (Zech 14; 2 Th 1:7-10; Jude 14-15; Rev 16:13-16; 19:11-21; Ezek 38-39).

8. At the rapture there will be no change of home lands on earth among the nations (Jn 14:1-3), while at the second advent there will be a general segregation of nations back to their original home lands, including Israel (Isa 11:11-12; Dt 32:8; Ezek 37; Mt 24:31; Acts 17:26).

9. At the rapture no man will be sent to hell, but all saints will be taken to heaven (Jn 14:1-3; Lk 21:34-36; 1 Th 4:16; Rev 5:8-10; 19:1-10), while at the second advent millions of men will be sent to hell and none taken to heaven (Mt 13:30, 43-50; 25:31-46; Isa 14:9-15; Rev 14:9-11; 19:20; 20:10).

10. At the rapture all saints will "escape all these things that shall come to pass" during the tribulation, and will "stand before the Son of man" (Lk 21:34-36; Jn 14:1-3; 1 Th 4:16; 5:1-11; Rev 5:8-10; 19:1-10. See Chapter 10) whereas, at the second advent no man who is subject to punishment will escape (Rev 19:1-21; Mt 24:29-31; 25:31-46; 2 Th 1:7-10).

11. The rapture will take place *before* the revelation of the Antichrist (2 Th 2:7-8) and *before* the tribulation and fulfillment of Rev 4:1-22:21, while the second advent will take place *after* these events (Mt 24:29-31; 2 Th 2:7-8; Rev 5:8-10; 19:11-21). See Chapter 10.

12. At the rapture there will be a resurrection of all the righteous dead (1 Th 4:16; 1 Cor 15:23, 51-54; Phil 3:21), while at the second advent there will be no resurrection of any righteous man, for the first resurrection will then be over (Rev 20:4-6).

13. At the time of the rapture no man on earth will know who the Antichrist is (2 Th 2:7-8) whereas, at the second advent all men on earth in the civilized parts will know who he is (Rev 13:16-18).

14. At the rapture the church and all others who are redeemed saints at that time will be presented to God in heaven (Eph 5:27; 1 Th 3:13; 5:23), while at the second advent all raptured saints will be presented to men on earth as their new rulers (Rev 2:27; 5:10; 20:4-6; Dan 7:9-27).

15. Before the rapture there will be no marriage supper of the Lamb whereas, just before the second advent there will be such a supper of Christ with all the redeemed of all ages past (Rev 19:1-21).

16. There will be a 7-year period of tribulation *after* the rapture (2 Th 2:7-8; Dan 9:27; Rev 6:1-19:21) whereas, there will be no tribulation at all after the second advent, for the second coming of Christ ends all tribulation (Mt 24:29-31; 25:31-46; Rev 19-20).

17. There will be no end of the world (age) at the time of the

rapture, while the age will definitely end at the time of the second advent of Christ to the earth (Mt 24:1-3, 29-31; 25:31-46; 2 Th 2:7-8; Rev 19:1-20:10).

18. The rapture is an event that can take place any day without any prophecy being fulfilled or any sign coming to pass (1 Cor 1:7; Phil 3:21; Tit 2:13; 1 Th 1:10) while the second advent cannot take place until all of the predictions in Mt 24-25; Mk 13; Lk 21:1-11, 25-33; 2 Th 2:7-8; Rev 4:1-19:10 have been fulfilled.

19. There will be no reign of the Antichrist *before* the rapture, but there will be such a reign before the second advent (Dan 9:27; 2 Th 2:7-8; Rev 6:1-19:21).

20. There will be no martyrdoms of saints after the second advent, while there will be multitudes of martyrs after the rapture and between the time of the rapture and the second advent (Rev 6:9-11; 7:9-17; 13:7; 14:9-13; 15:1-4; 17:6; 18:24; 20:4-6).

We conclude then, that IF the church and all other raptured saints are to eat a marriage supper with Christ in heaven, as in Rev 19:1-10, which happens just before the second advent begins, as in Rev 19:11-21, then the church cannot remain on earth through the tribulation period. It must arrive in heaven prior to the time of the second advent. Furthermore, IF the saints are to leave WITH Christ at the second advent they must already be up in heaven BEFORE that time so as to be able to return WITH Him. And IF – rather SINCE the rapture can take place at any moment as taught in 1 Cor 15:51-54; Phil 3:21 and Tit 2:13 – since it could have happened even in Paul's day according to these passages of Scripture – then we can be certain that the rapture will not take place at a specified time as in the case of the second advent which is predicted to happen at a particular time, that is, at the end of the tribulation period (Mt 24:29-31; Rev 19:11-21). This, to us, is truly conclusive proof that the rapture of the church and O. T. saints will take place BEFORE the tribulation begins.

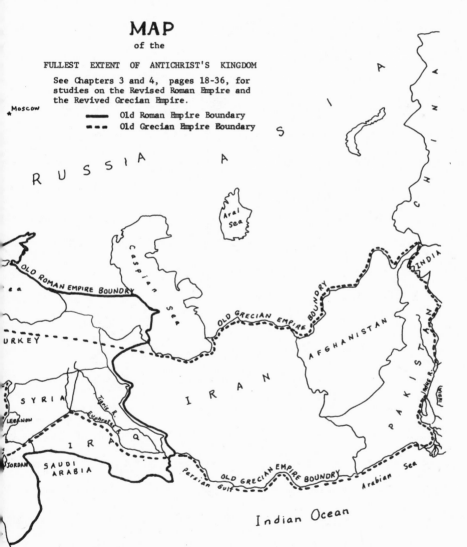

MAP

of the

FULLEST EXTENT OF ANTICHRIST'S KINGDOM

See Chapters 3 and 4, pages 18-36, for studies on the Revised Roman Empire and the Revived Grecian Empire.

──── Old Roman Empire Boundary
▬ ▬ ▬ Old Grecian Empire Boundary